Of Menus and Mythology

Late Nineteenth-Century Print Graphics

by Symbolist Master

Franz von Stuck

Dover Publications, Inc.
Mineola, New York

Bibliographical Note

This Dover edition, first published in 2017, is an unabridged republication of *Cartes et Vignettes*, originally published by Gerlach and Schenk, Vienna, in 1890.

Library of Congress Cataloging-in-Publication Data

Names: Stuck, Franz von, 1863–1928, artist.
Title: Of menus and mythology : late nineteenth-century print graphics / Franz von Stuck.
Other titles: Karten und Vignetten
Description: Mineola, New York : Dover Publications, Inc. 2017. | "This Dover edition, first published in 2017, is an unabridged republication of the work originally published by Gerlach and Schenk, Vienna, in 1890."
Identifiers: LCCN 2017003973 | ISBN 9780486815909 (paperback) | ISBN 0486815900
Subjects: LCSH: Stuck, Franz von, 1863–1928—Themes, motives. | BISAC: ART /European.
Classification: LCC NC999.6.G3 S78 2017 | DDC 741.6—dc23 LC record available at https://lccn.loc.gov/2017003973

Manufactured in the United States by LSC Communications
81590001 2017
www.doverpublications.com

KARTEN

UND

VIGNETTEN

HERAUSGEGEBEN VON

MARTIN GERLACH.

ENTWÜRFE UND COMPOSITIONS-MOTIVE

FÜR

WEINKARTEN, MENUS, HOCHZEITSBLATTER, GLÜCKWUNSCHKARTEN,
PROGRAMME UND EINLADUNGEN ZU MUSIK-, GESANGS- ODER BALLFESTEN, ZUR JAGD ETC.;
FESTKARTEN FÜR DEN EIS-, WETTRENN-, VELOCIPED-, TURN-, KEGEL- UND SONSTIGEN SPORT

NEBST

EINEM CYKLUS HUMORISTISCHER

VIGNETTEN.

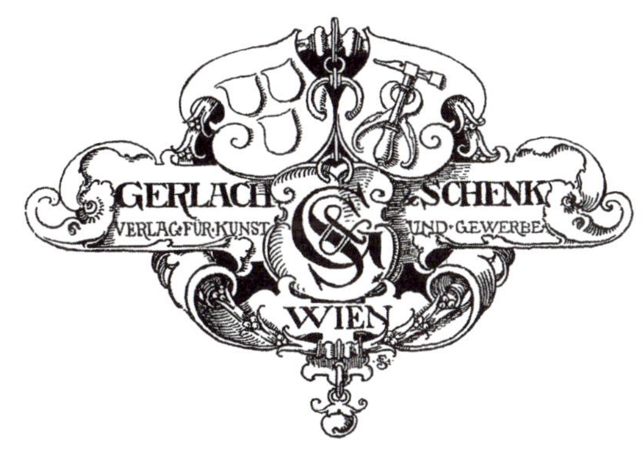

ORIGINAL-ZEICHNUNGEN VON F. STUCK, MUNCHEN.
ZINKOGRAPHIE VON G. MEISENBACH, MÜNCHEN. — DRUCK VON FRIEDRICH JASPER, WIEN.
PAPIER AUS DEN FABRIKEN VON EICHMANN & CIE., ARNAU, WIEN, PRAG.

[Original title page]

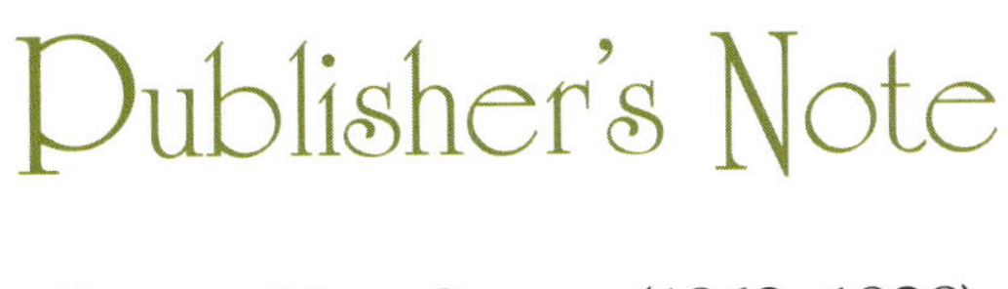

Publisher's Note

FRANZ VON STUCK (1863–1928) was an important figure in the late-nineteenth-century Symbolist movement, a gathering of literary and artistic ideas and works that originated with French poets such as Baudelaire, Mallarme, and Verlaine. The use of symbolism—identified with themes and motifs of fantasy and dreams, sensuality and eroticism, and, especially, myth and legend—in the arts was a reaction against the rigid formalism prevalent at the time. Von Stuck, a skilled engraver, painter, sculptor, architect, and caricaturist, was prodigious and highly accomplished: he produced the graphics included in this collection at the age of twenty-seven and became a professor at the Munich Academy of the Arts when in his early thirties (Paul Klee and Wassily Kandinsky were two of his notable students).

Of Menus and Mythology consists of rare graphic works that Von Stuck produced as "stock art" for diverse uses—menus, wine lists, and performance sheets. The striking imagery includes depictions of Dionysus and Bacchus, the Greek and Roman gods of wine; musical instruments; a cornucopia; cupids and cherubs; and scenes of rampant merriment and pleasure.

Of Menus and Mythology

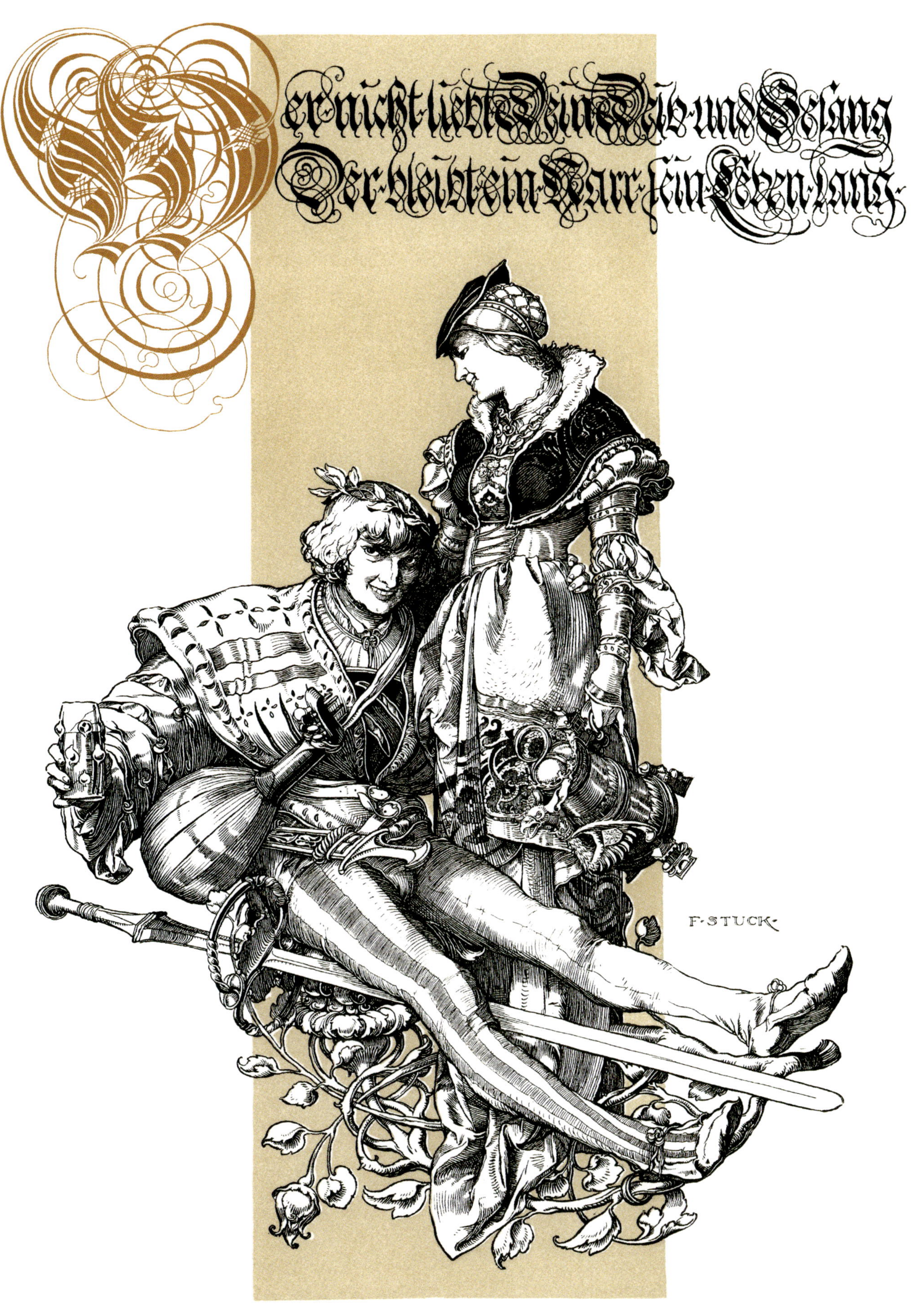
Wer·nicht·liebt·Wein·Weib·und·Gesang
Der·bleibt·ein·Narr·sein·Leben·lang·
F·STUCK·

PLATE 1

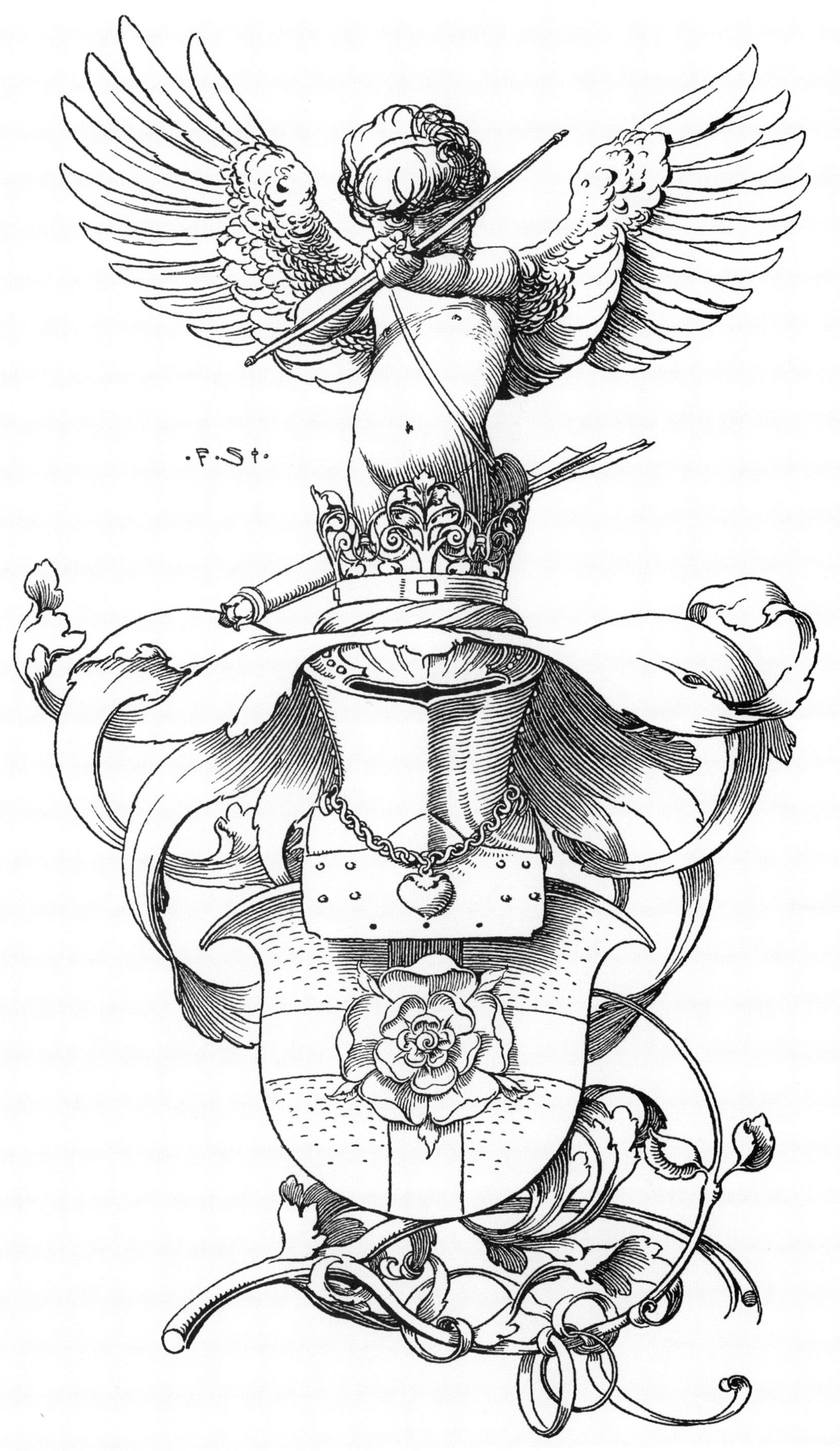

PLATE 2

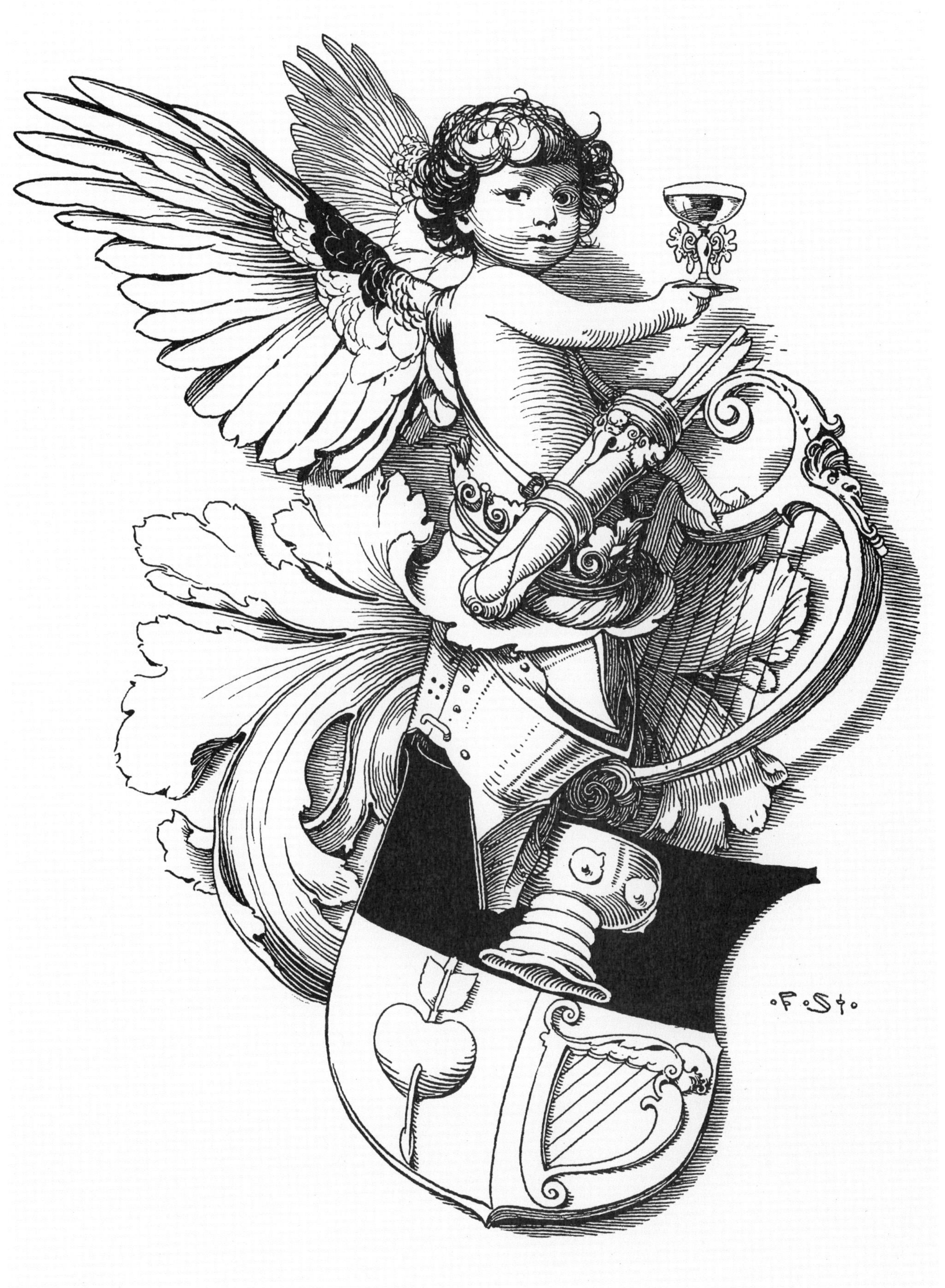
·F·S·

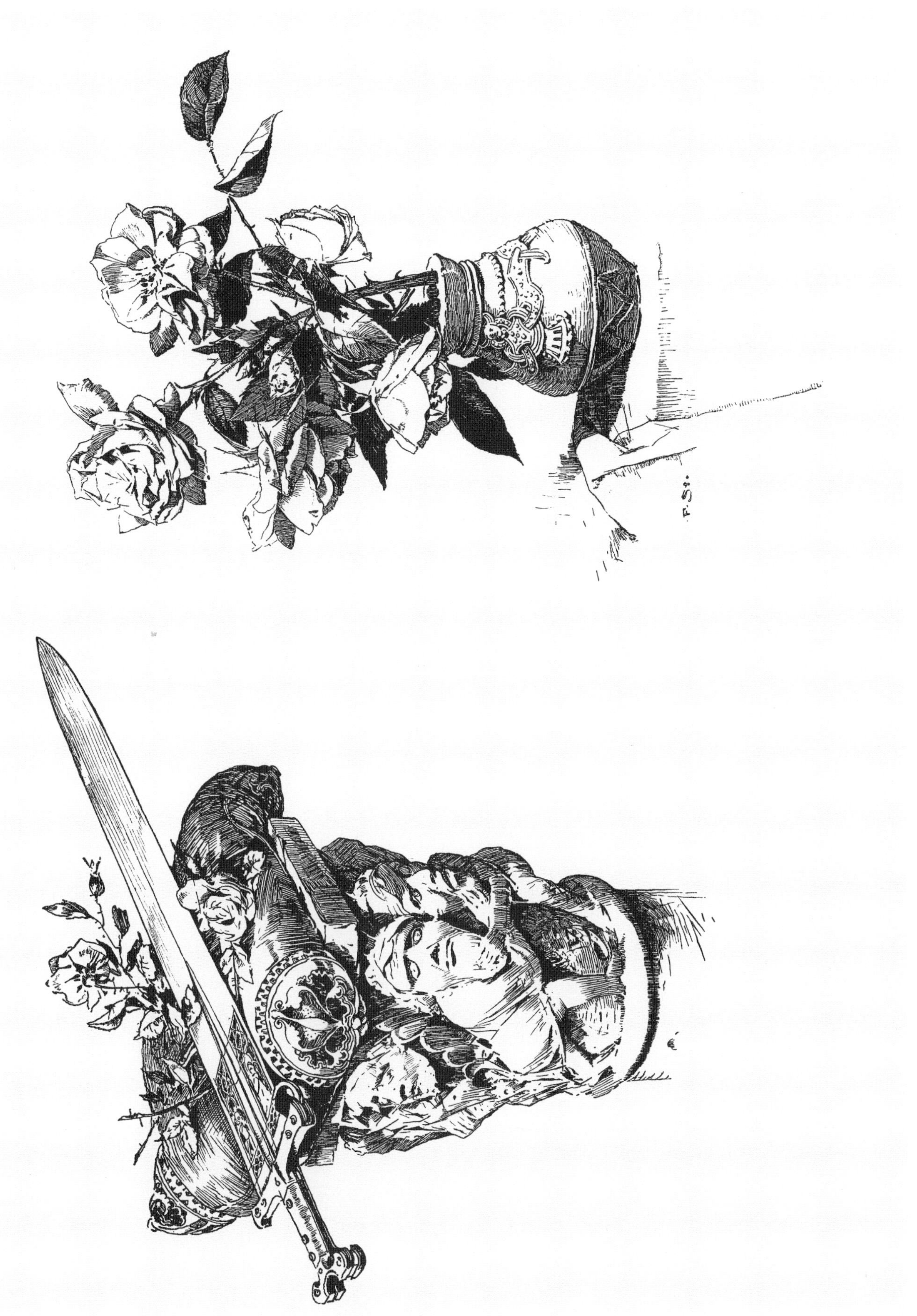

Plate 4

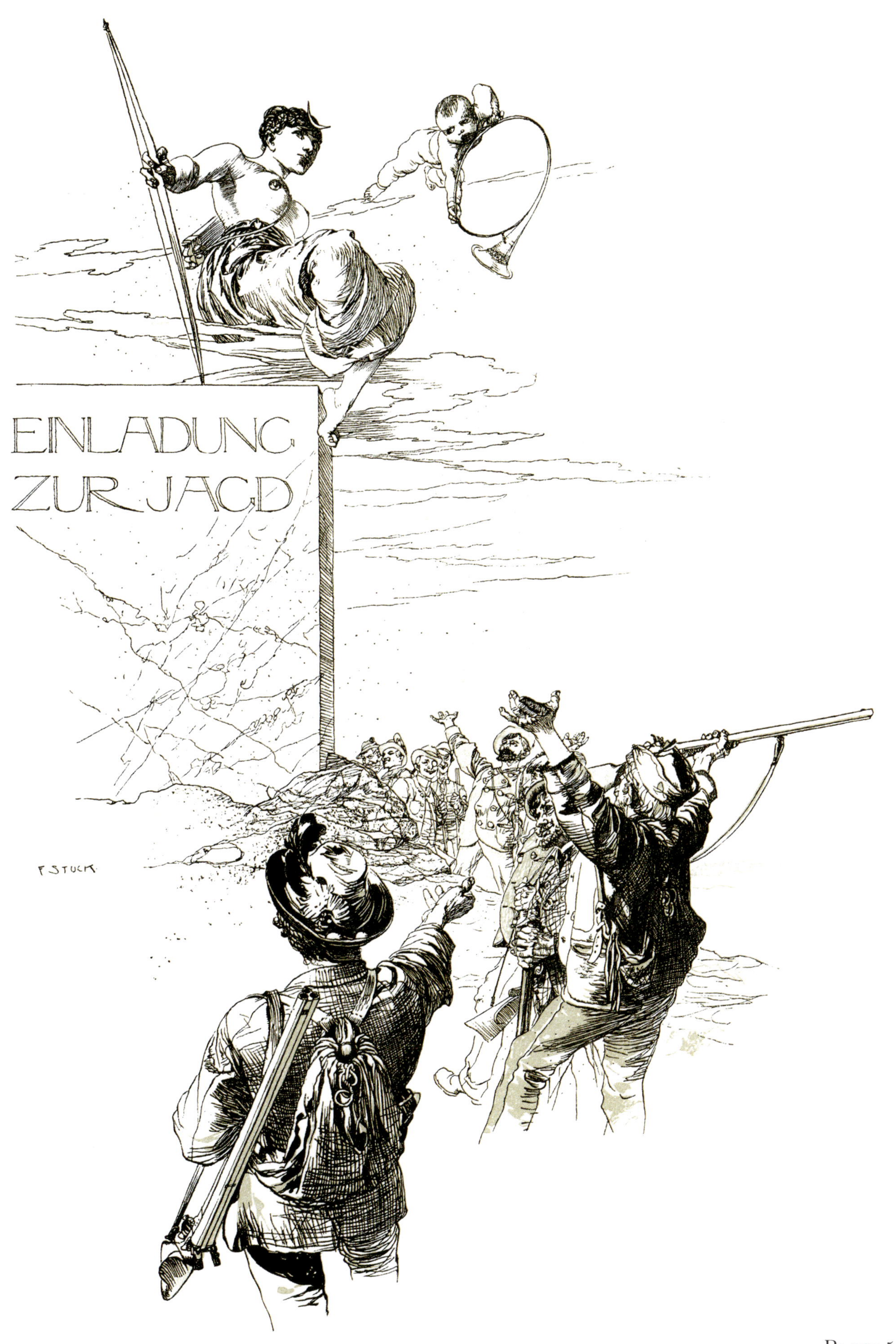
EINLADUNG
ZUR JAGD
F STUCK

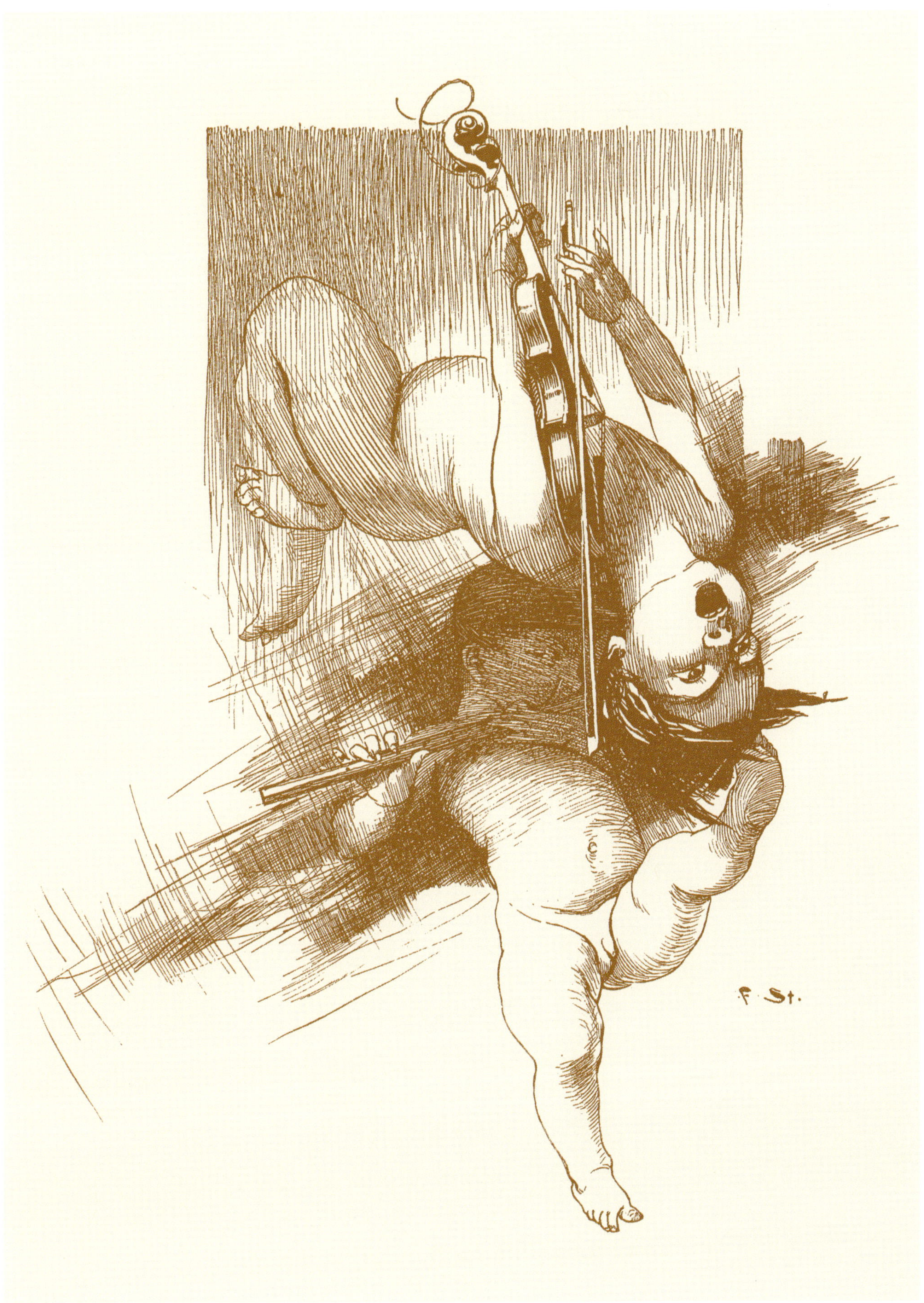

Plate 6

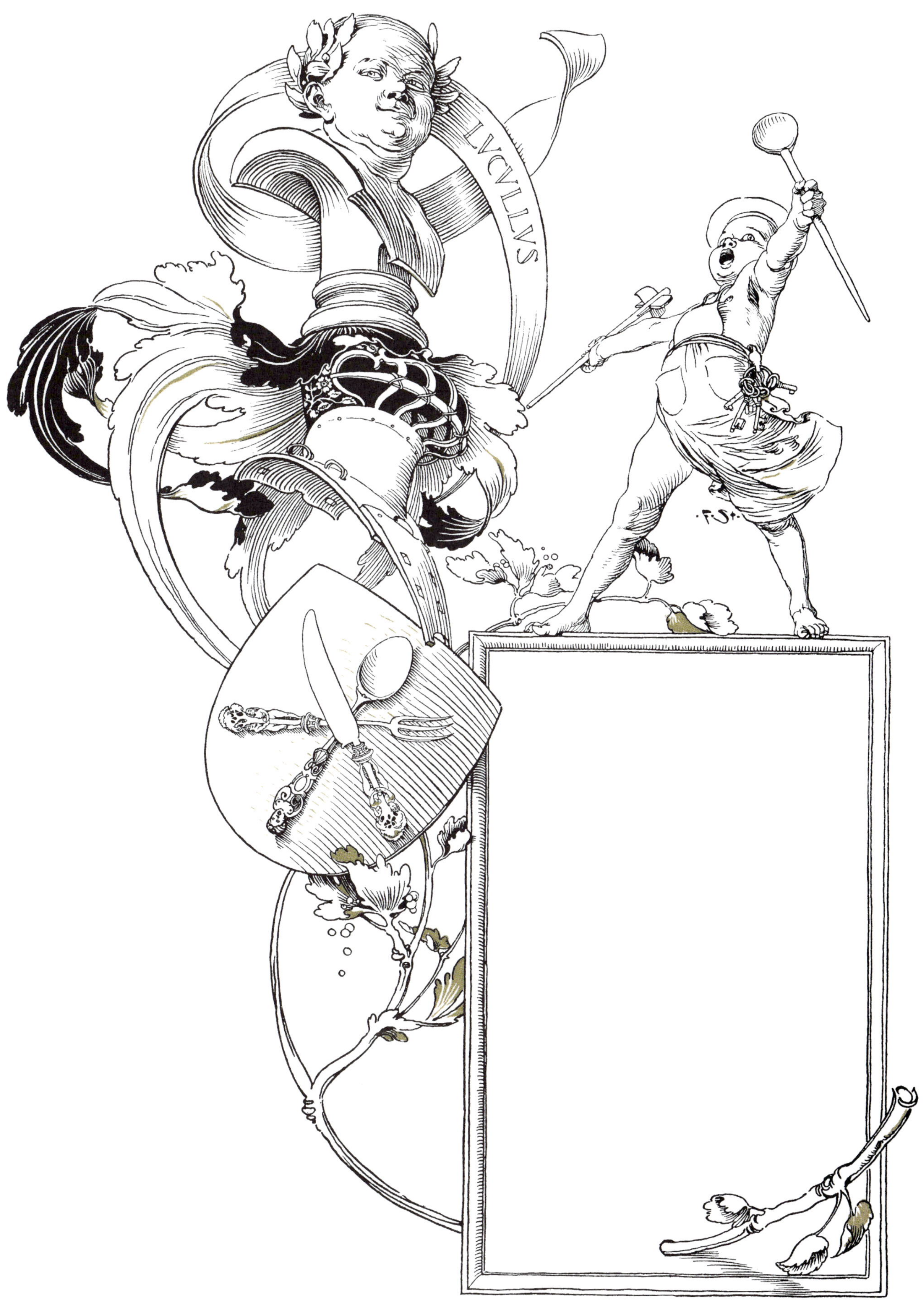

PLATE 7

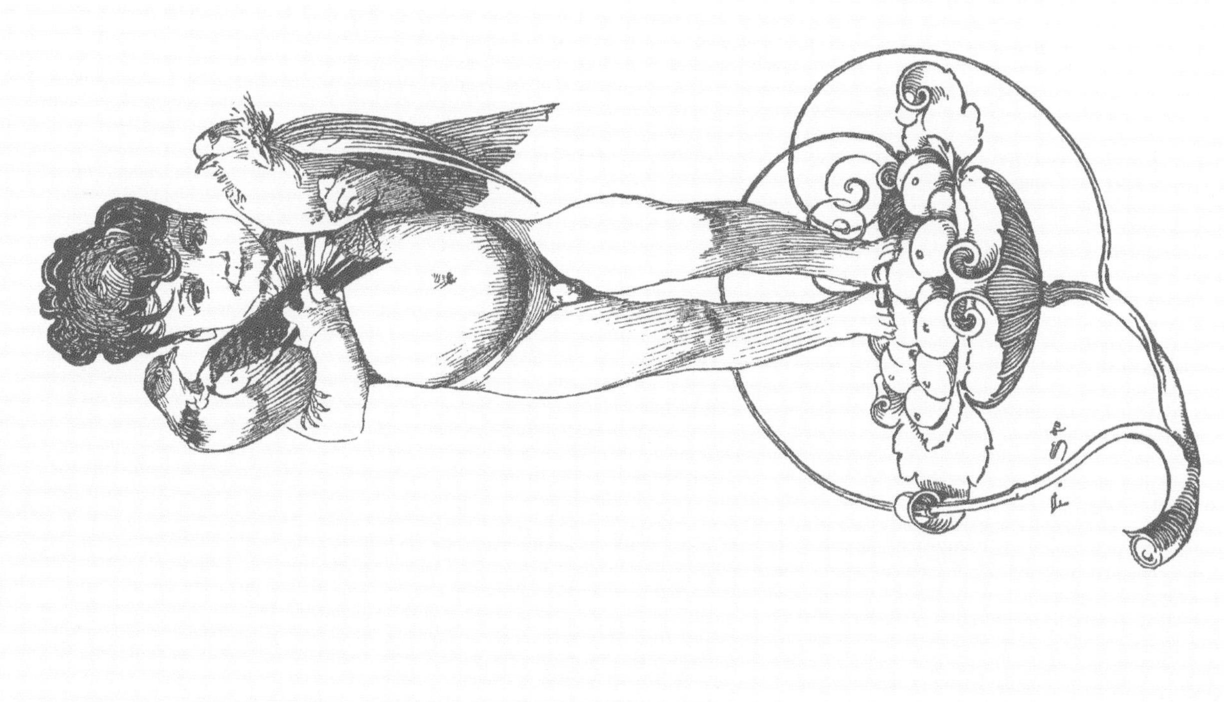

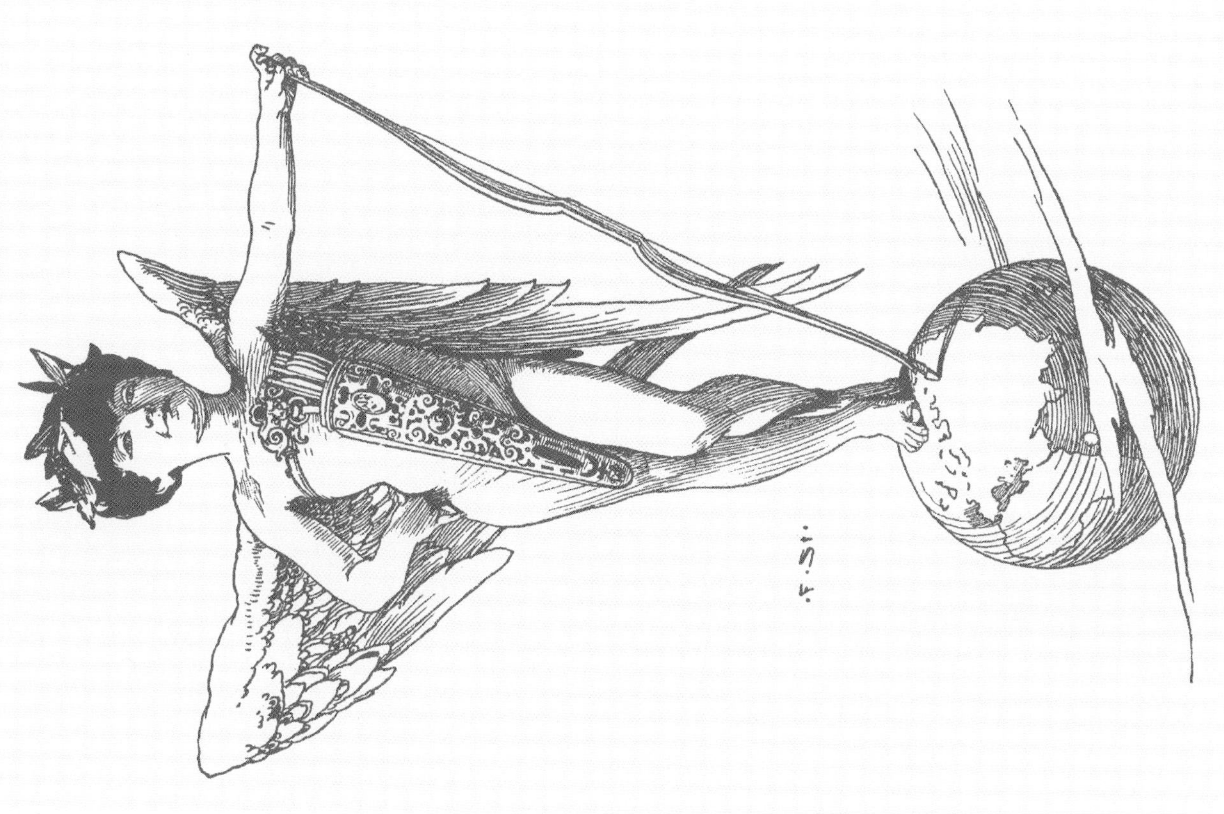

PLATE 8

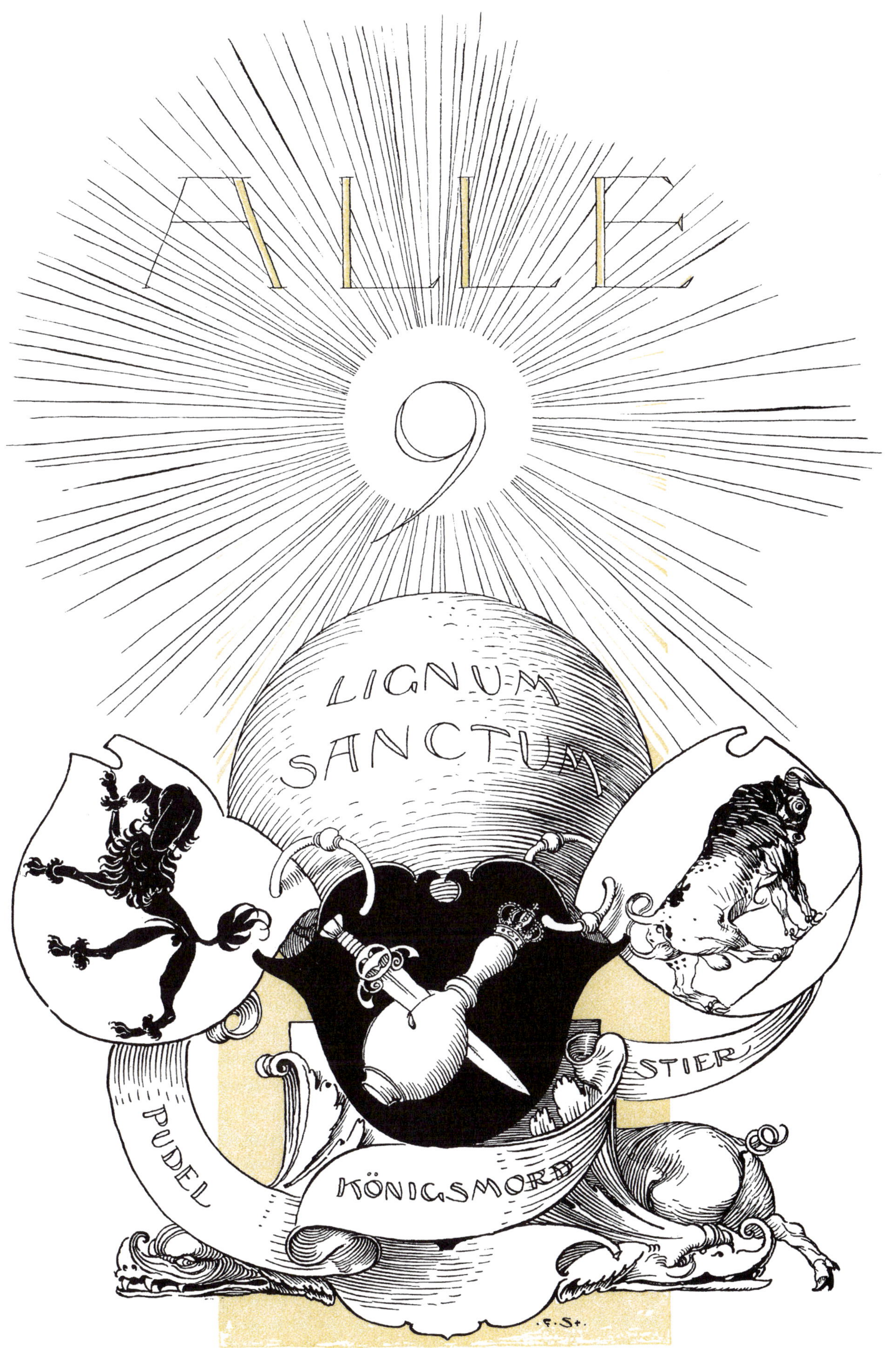
ALLE
9
LIGNUM
SANCTUM
STIER
PUDEL
KÖNIGSMORD
F. St.

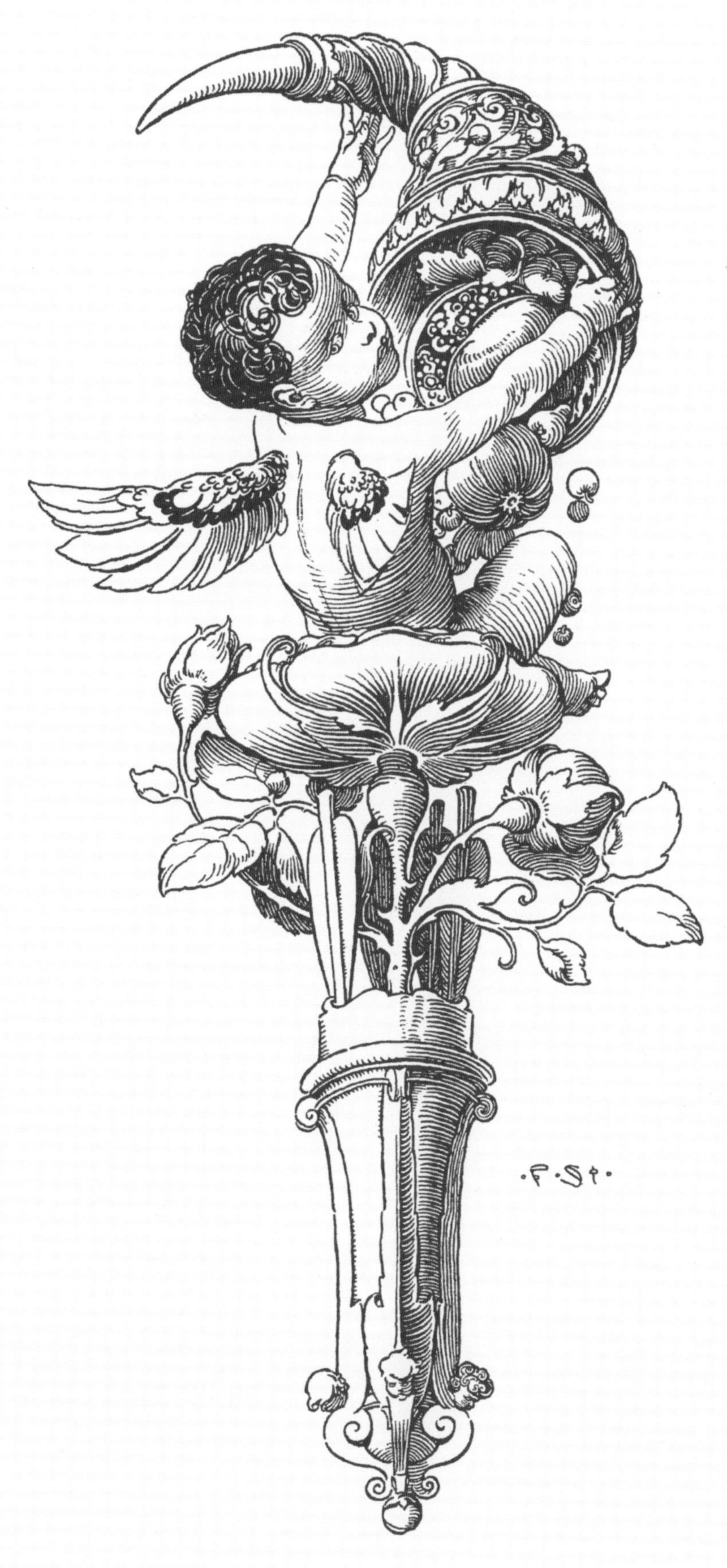

PLATE 10

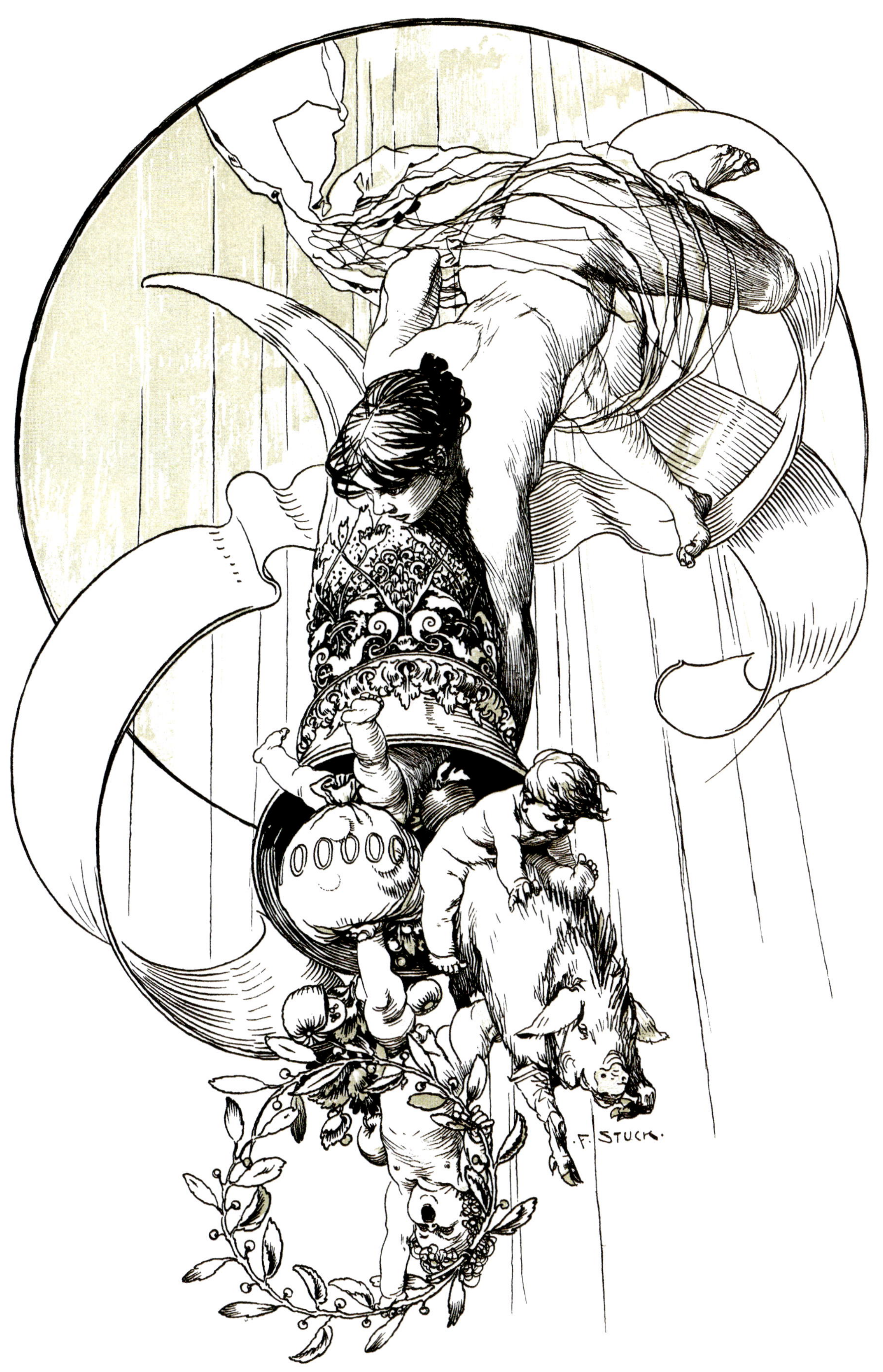

PLATE 11

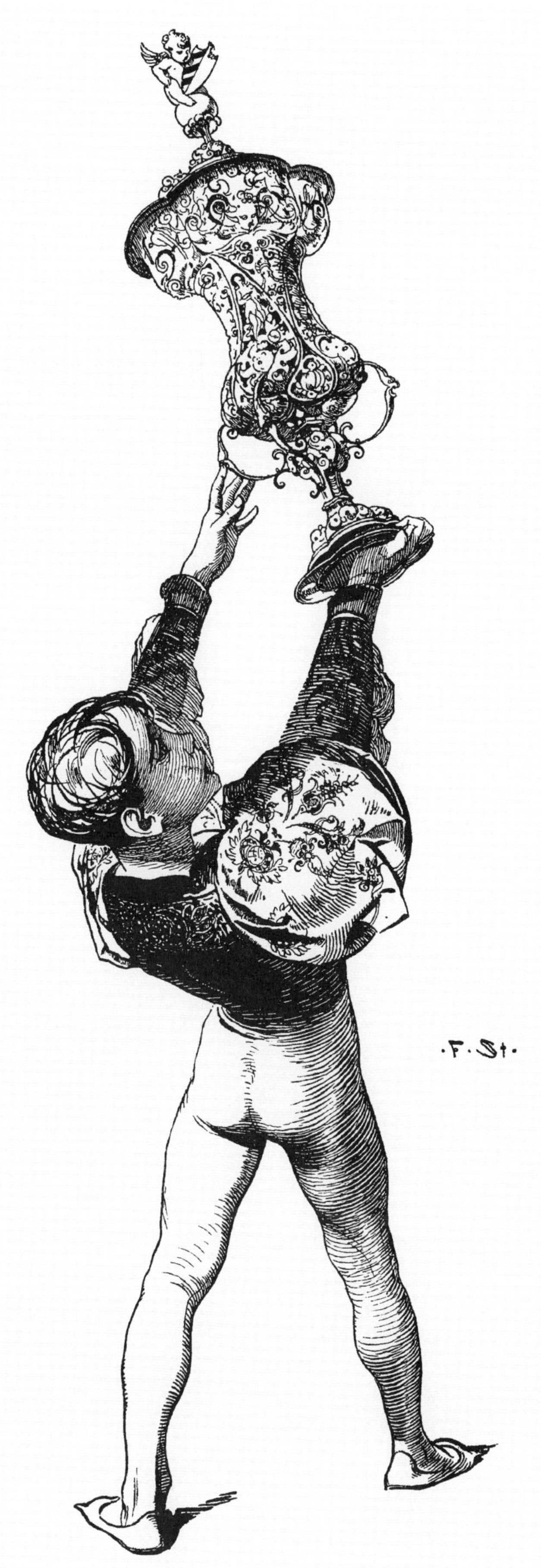

PLATE 12

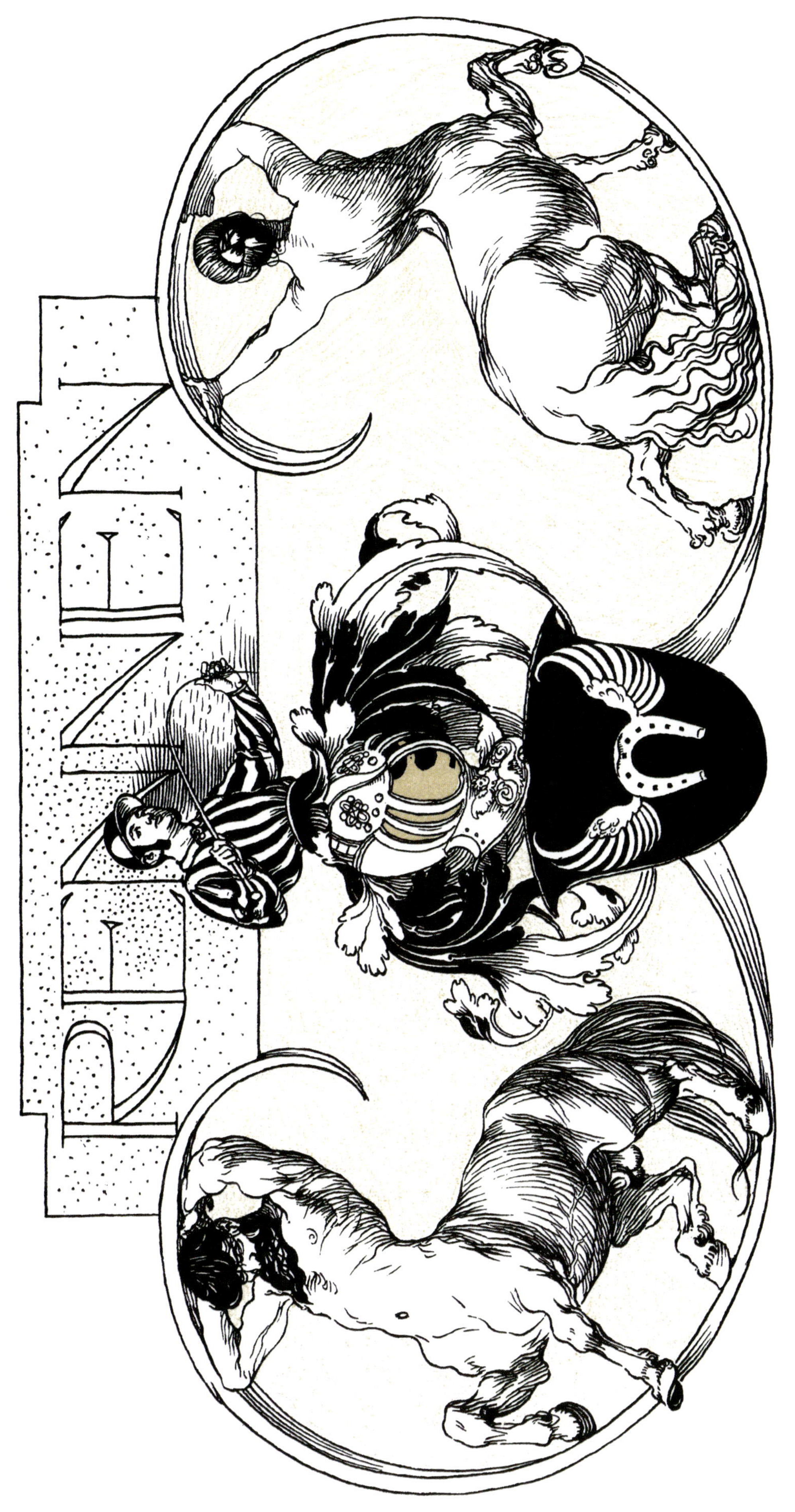

Plate 13

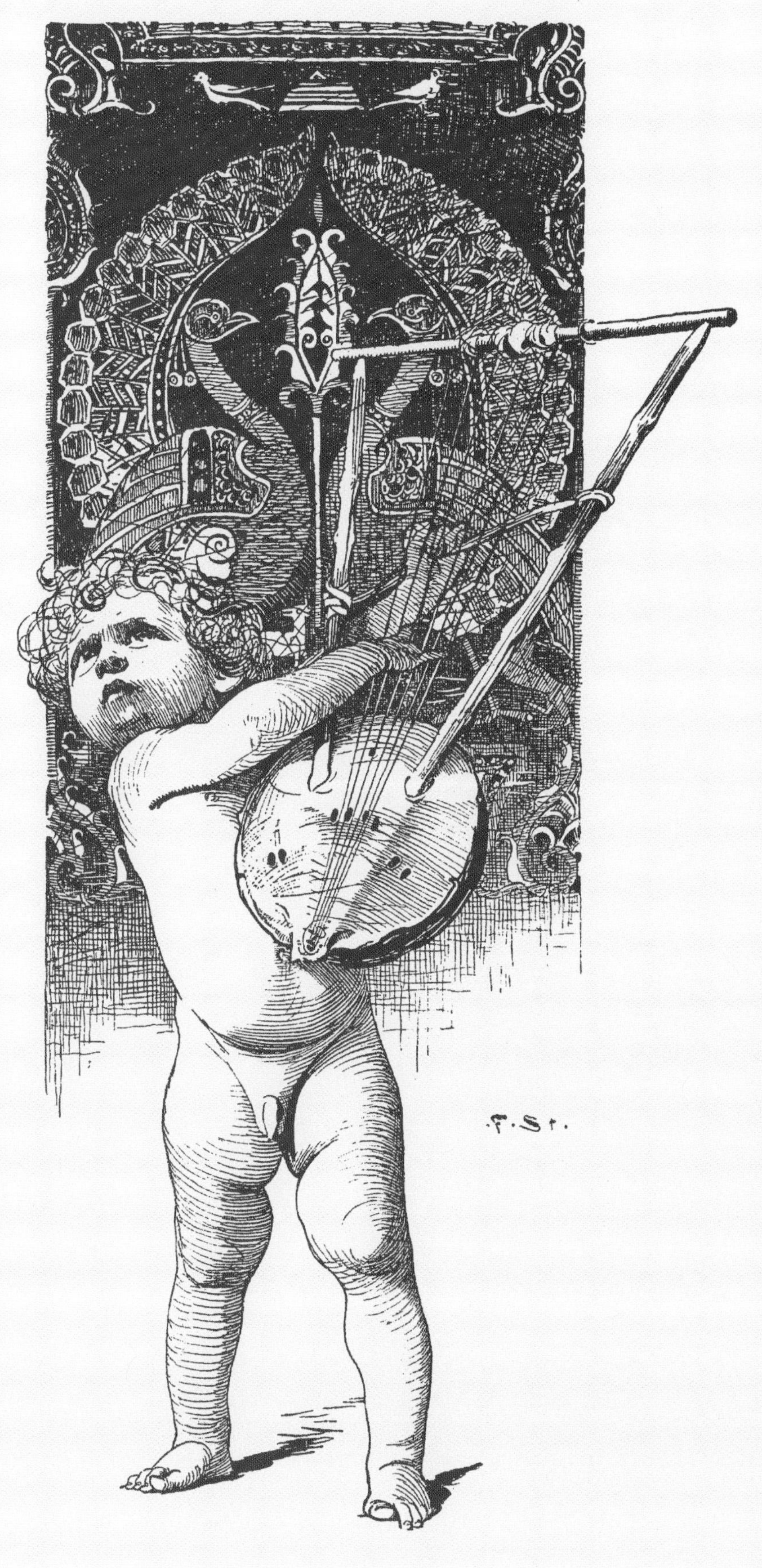

Plate 14

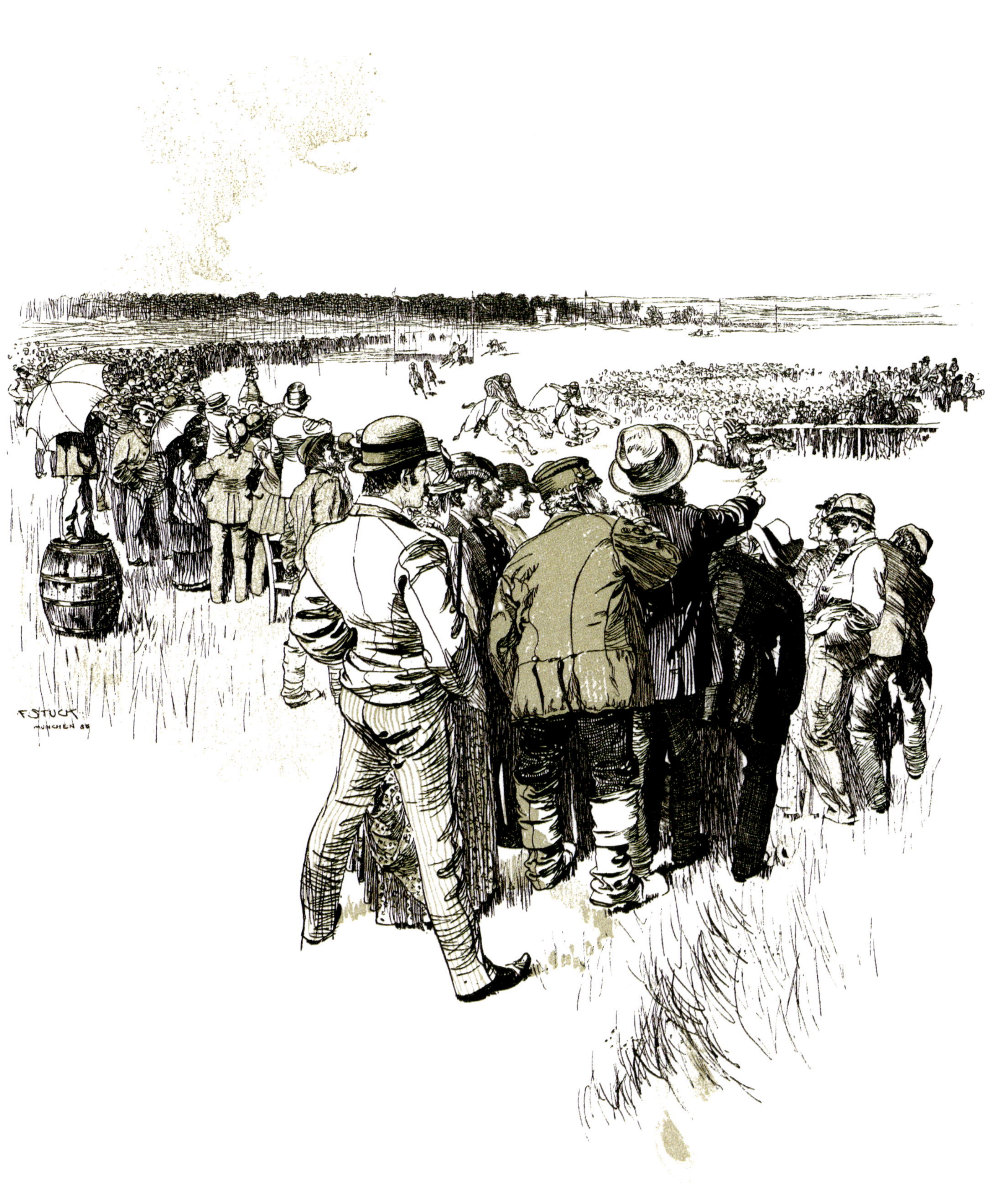

Plate 15

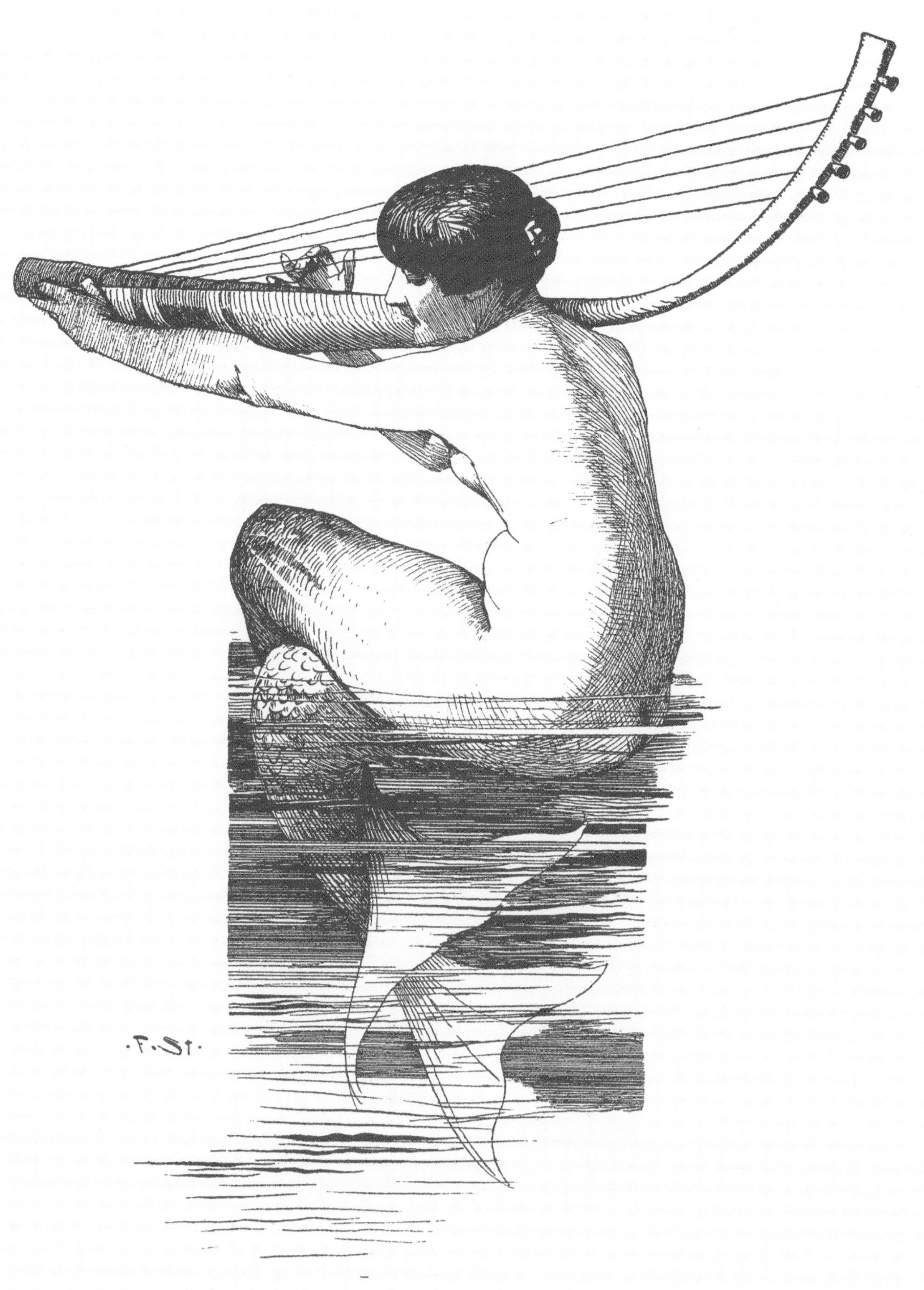

PLATE 16

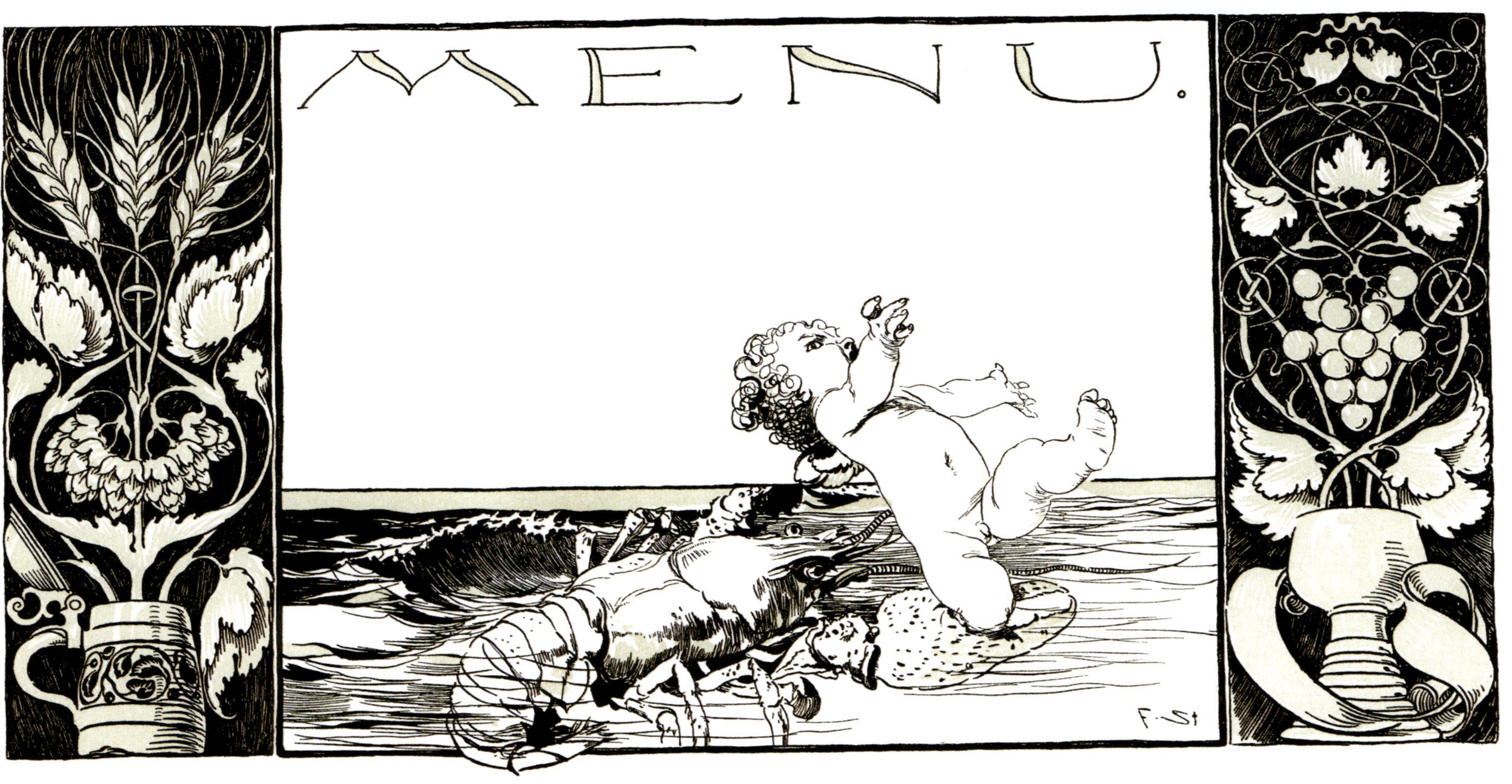

PLATE 17

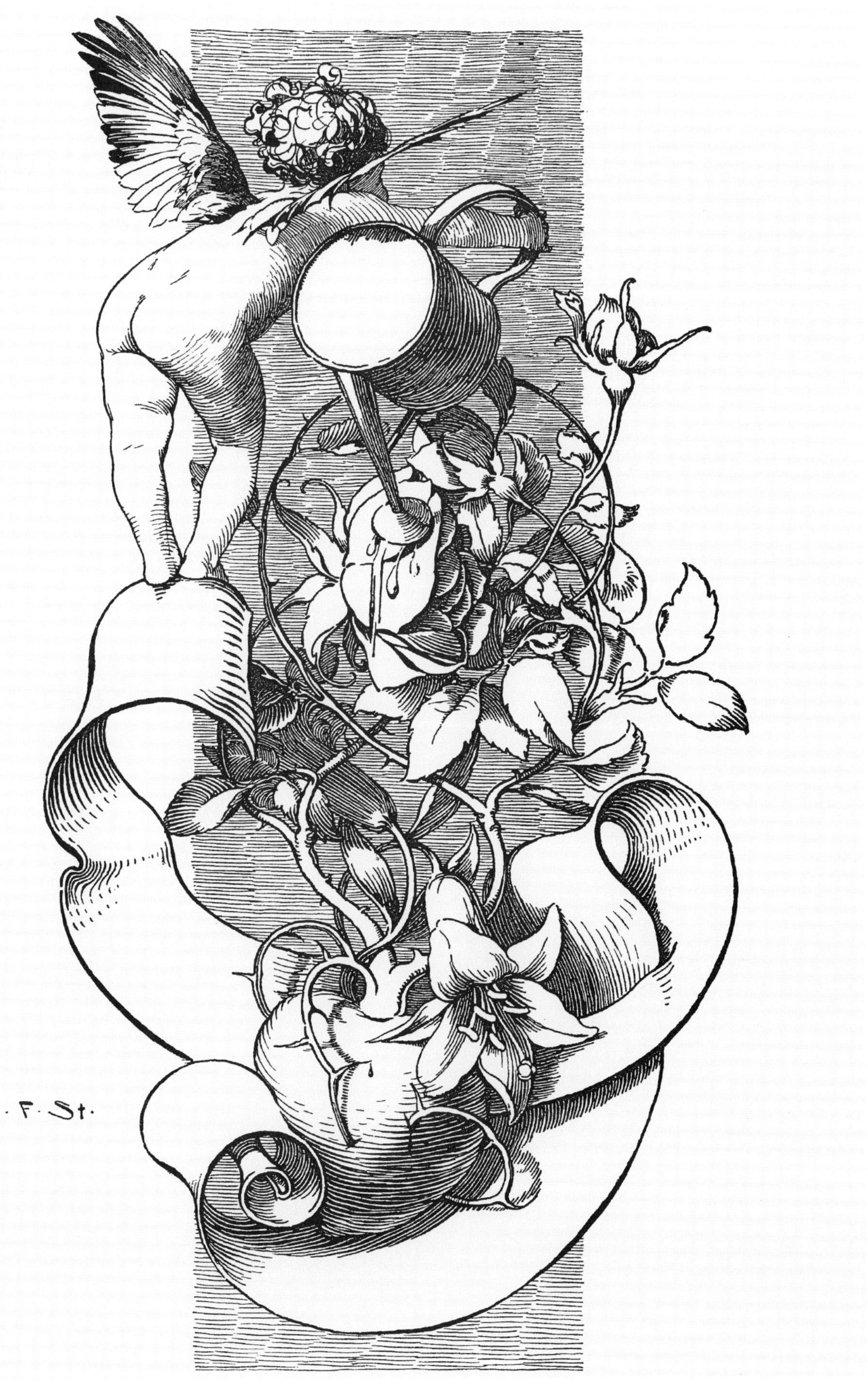

PLATE 18

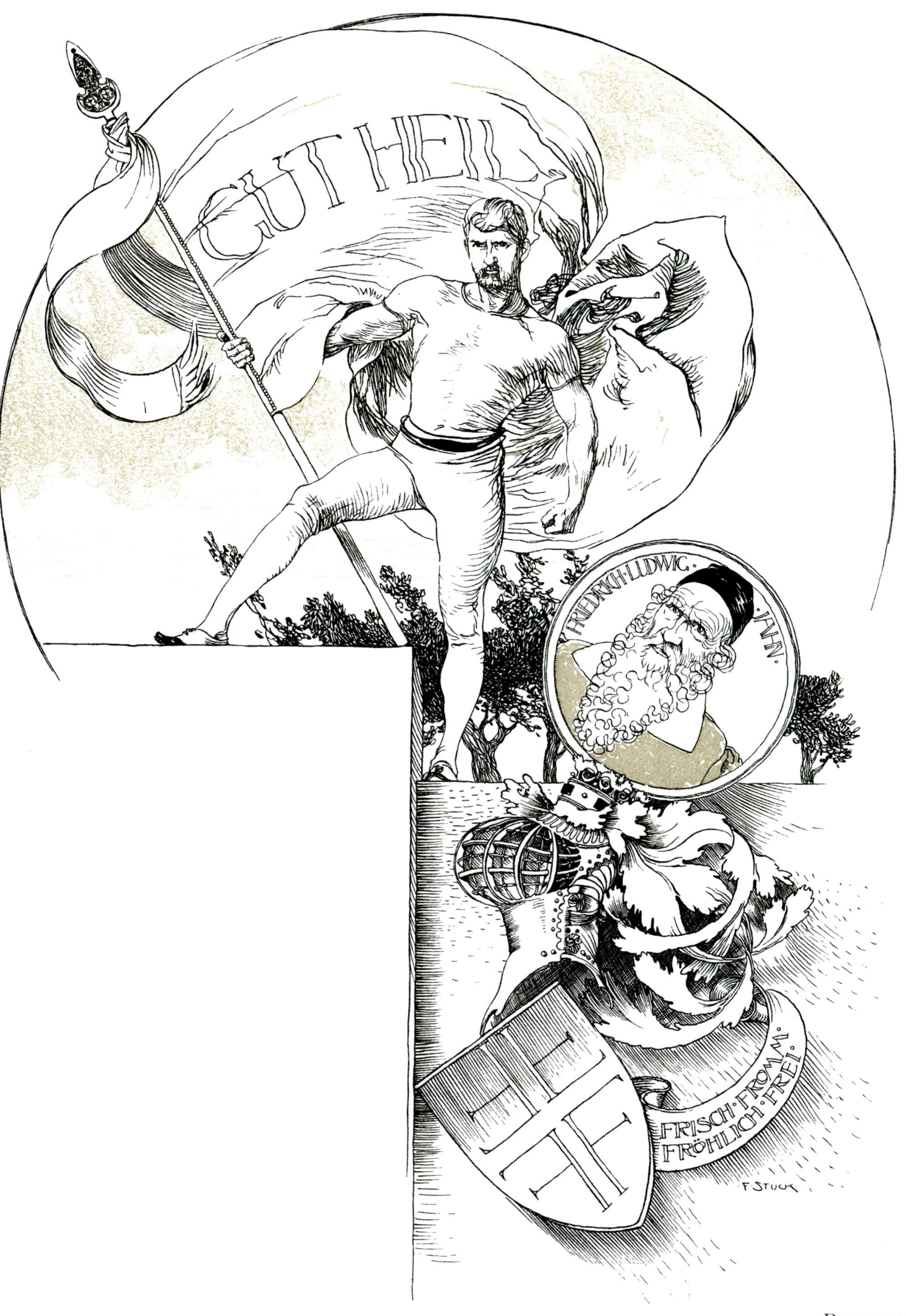
GUT HEIL
FRIEDRICH·LUDWIG·JAHN·
FRISCH·FROMM·
FRÖHLICH·FREI·
F·STUCK

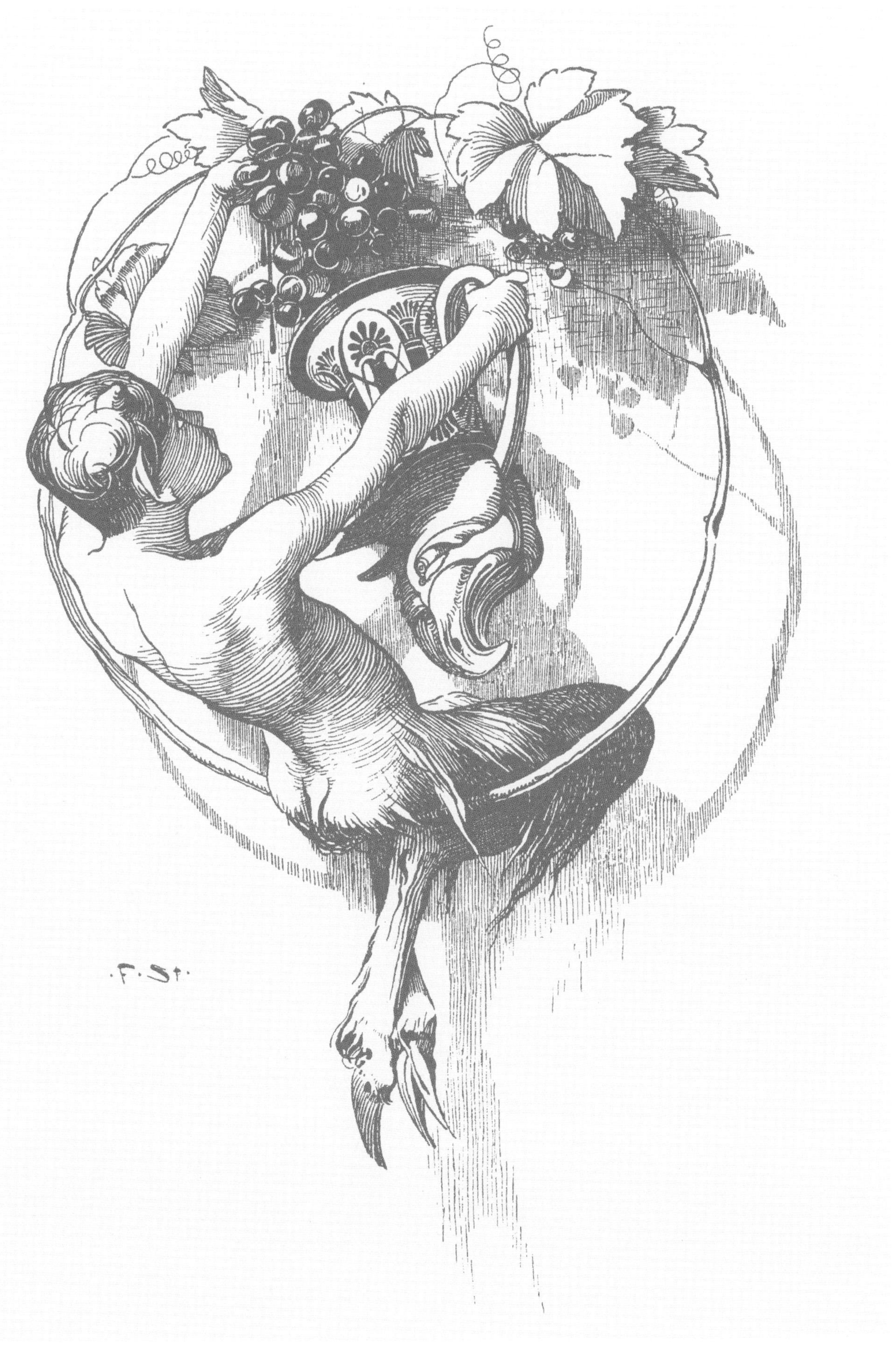
·F·St·

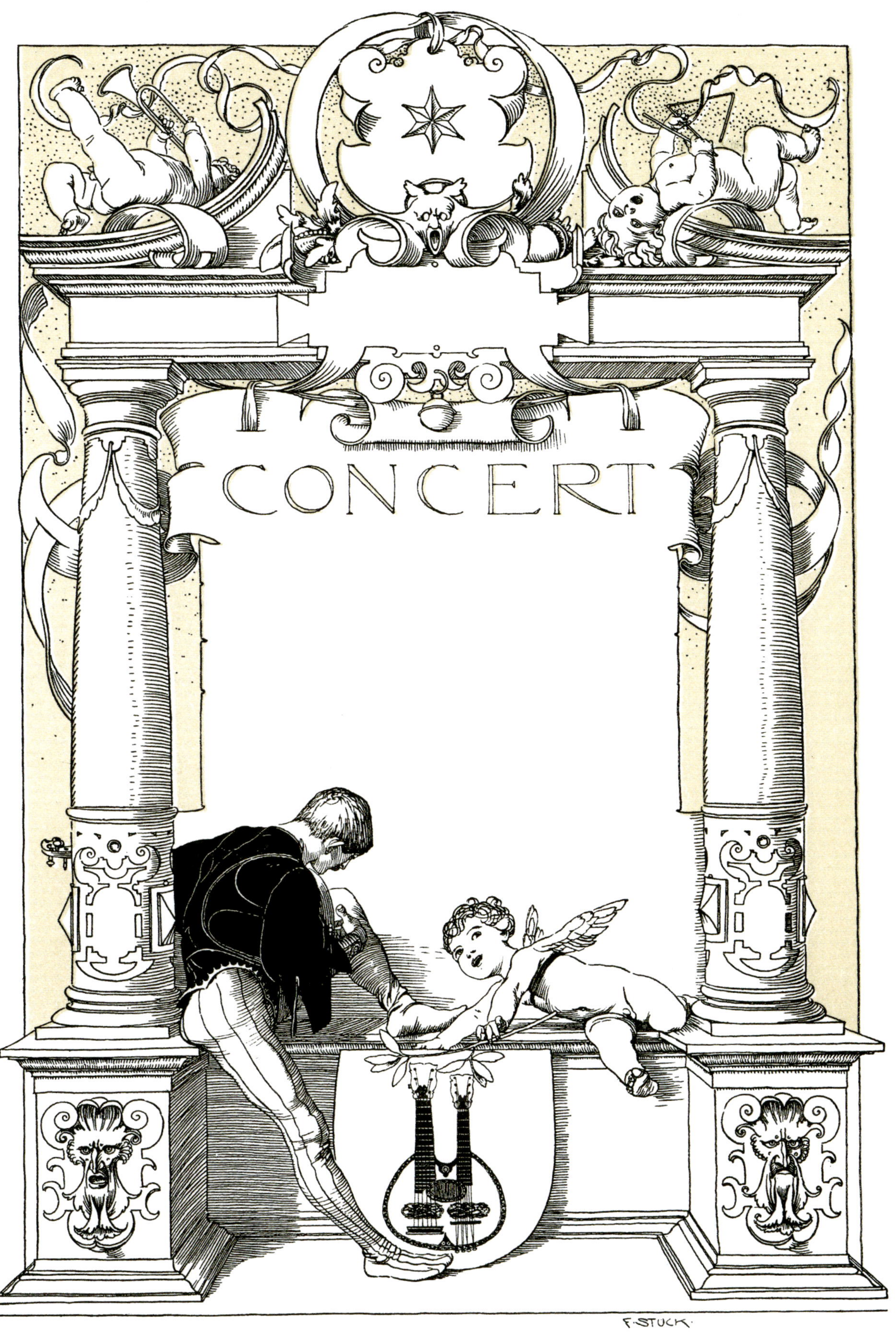
CONCERT
F. STUCK

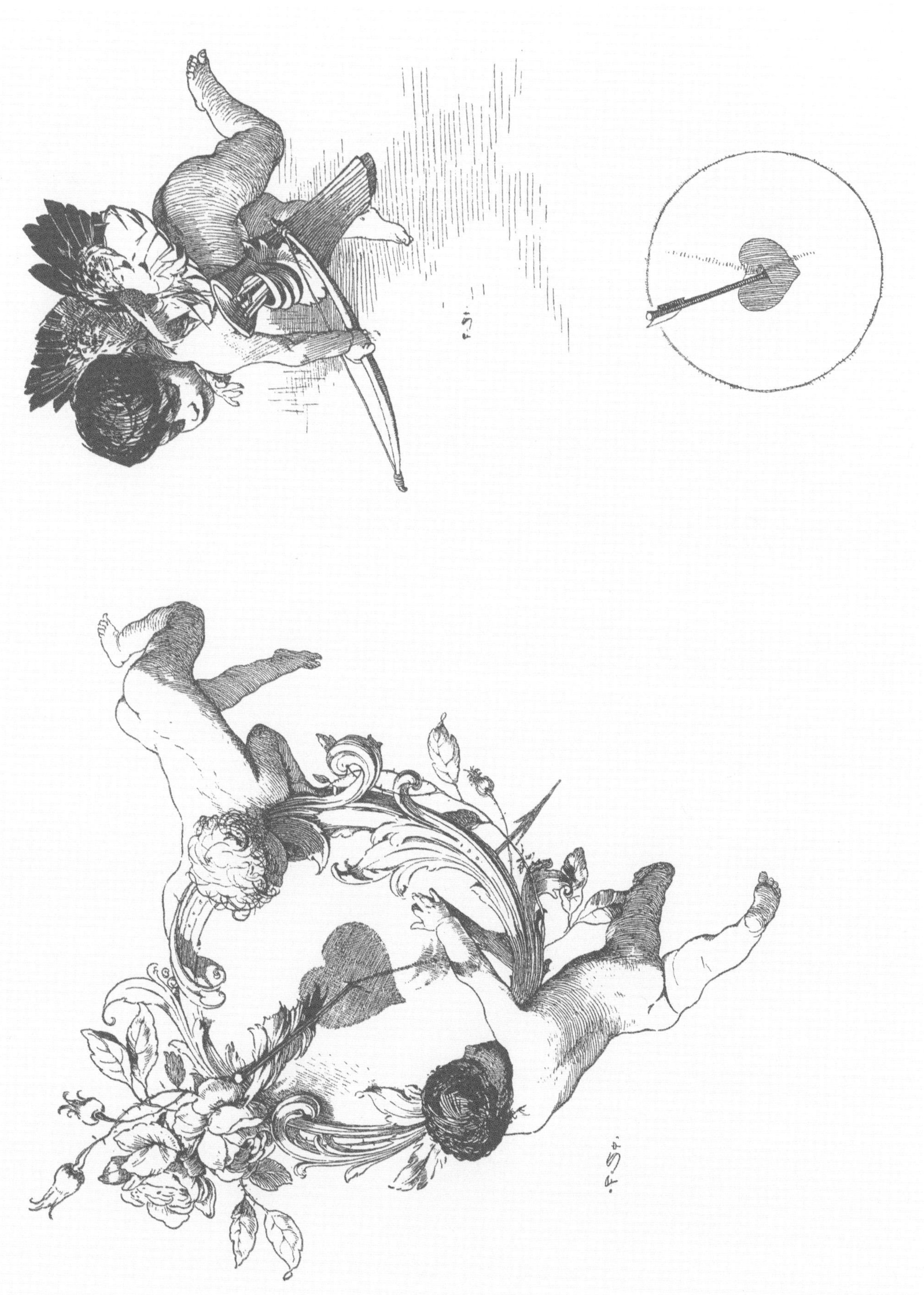

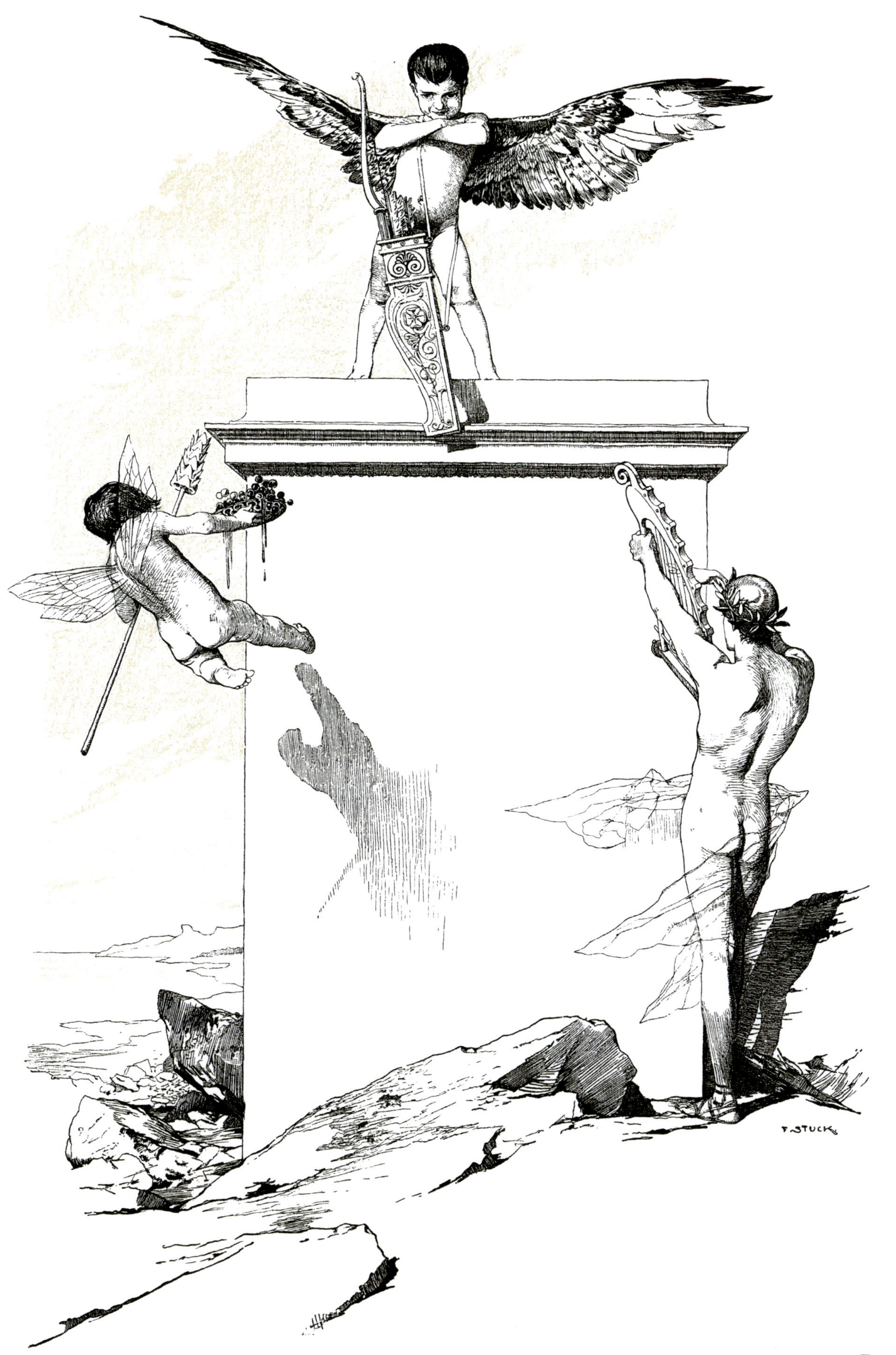

PLATE 23

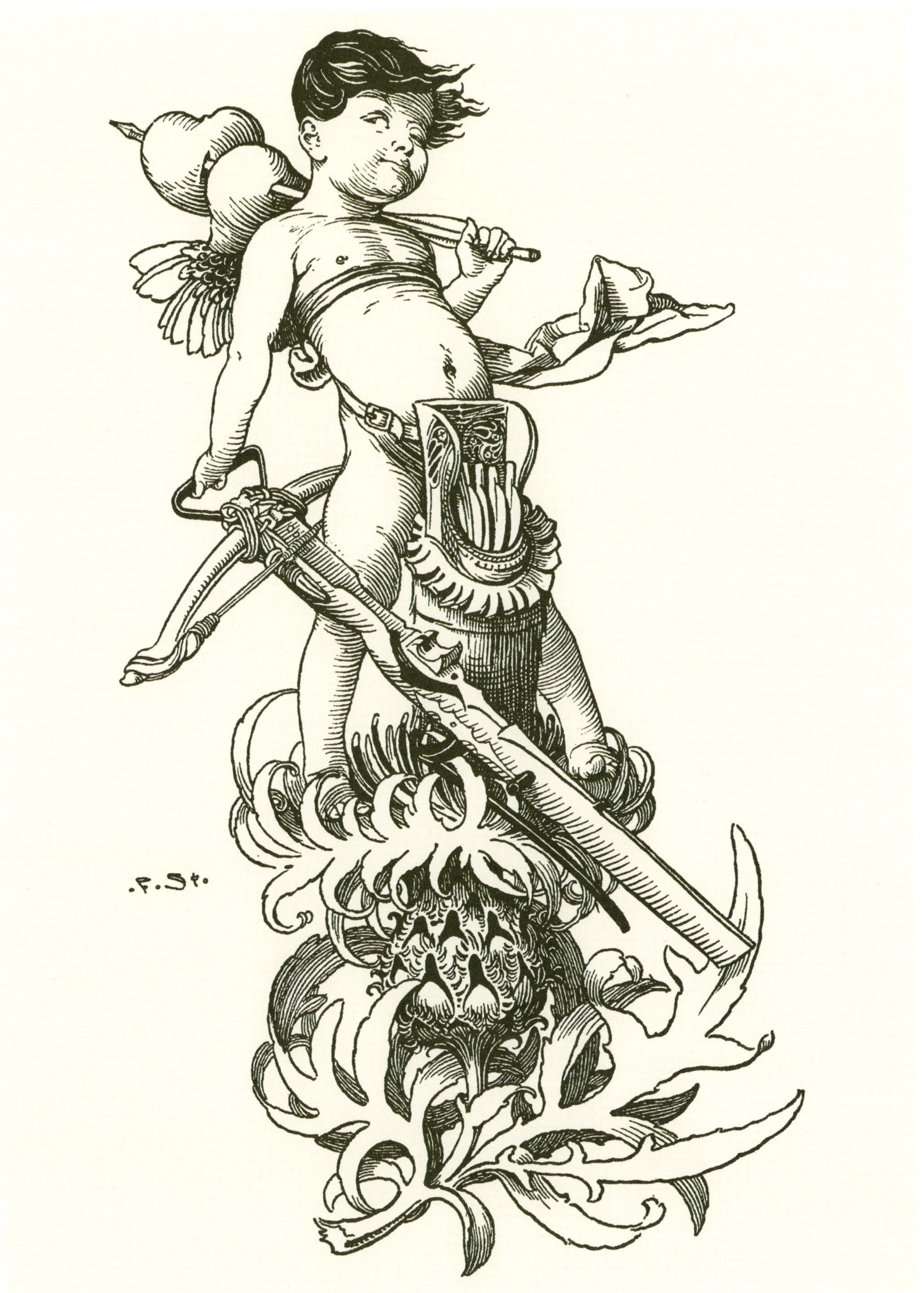

PLATE 24

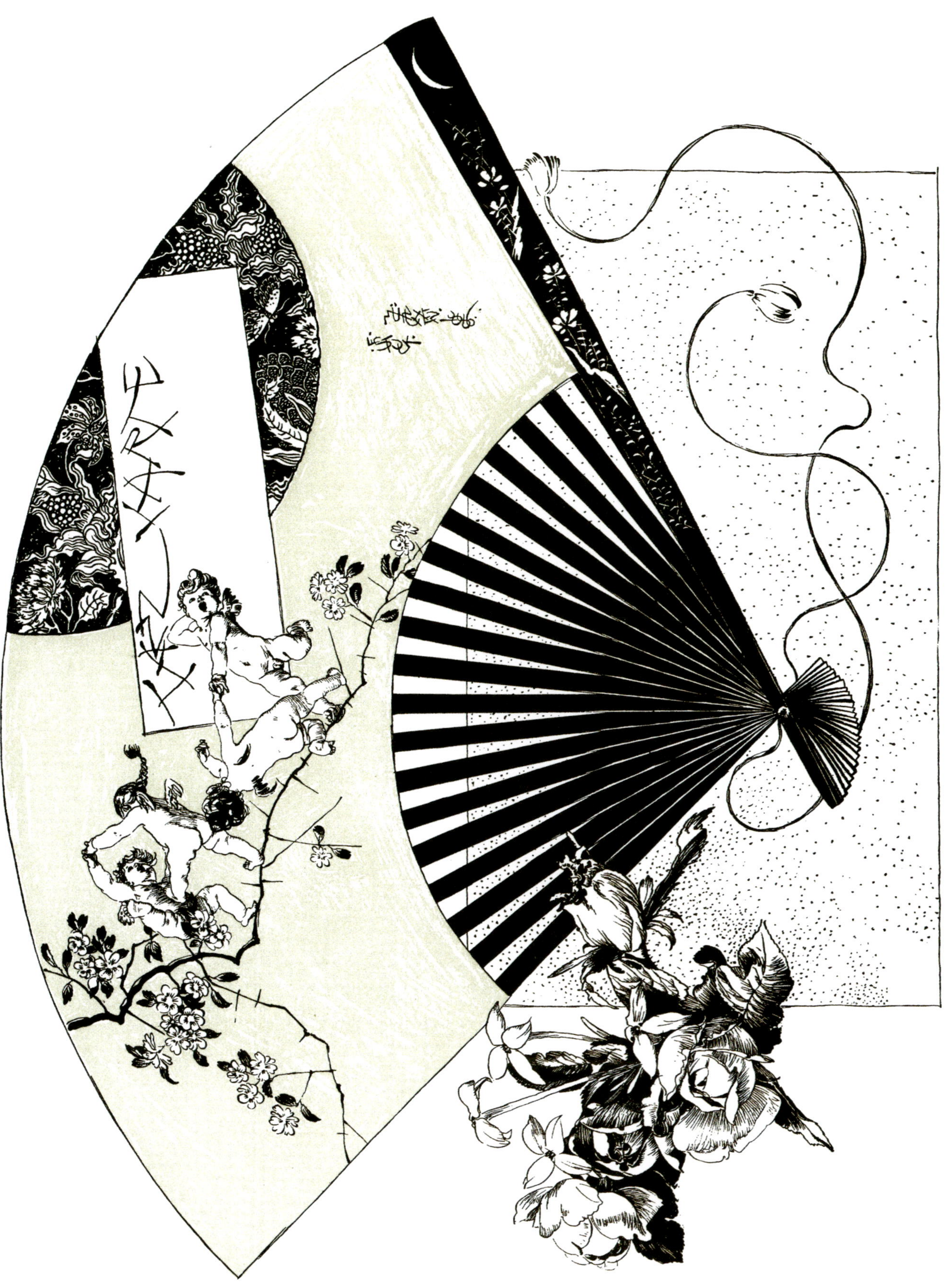

Plate 25

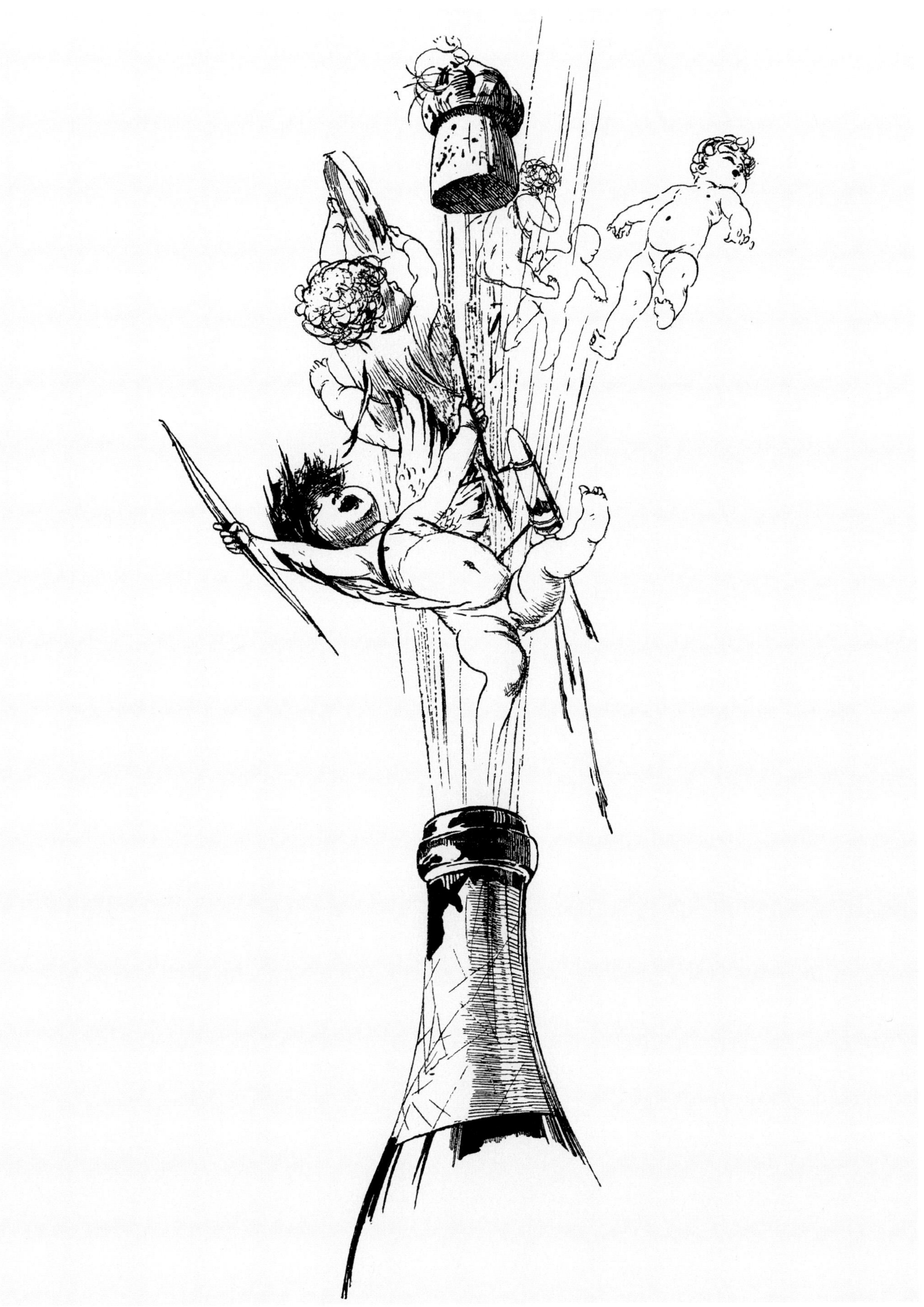

PLATE 26

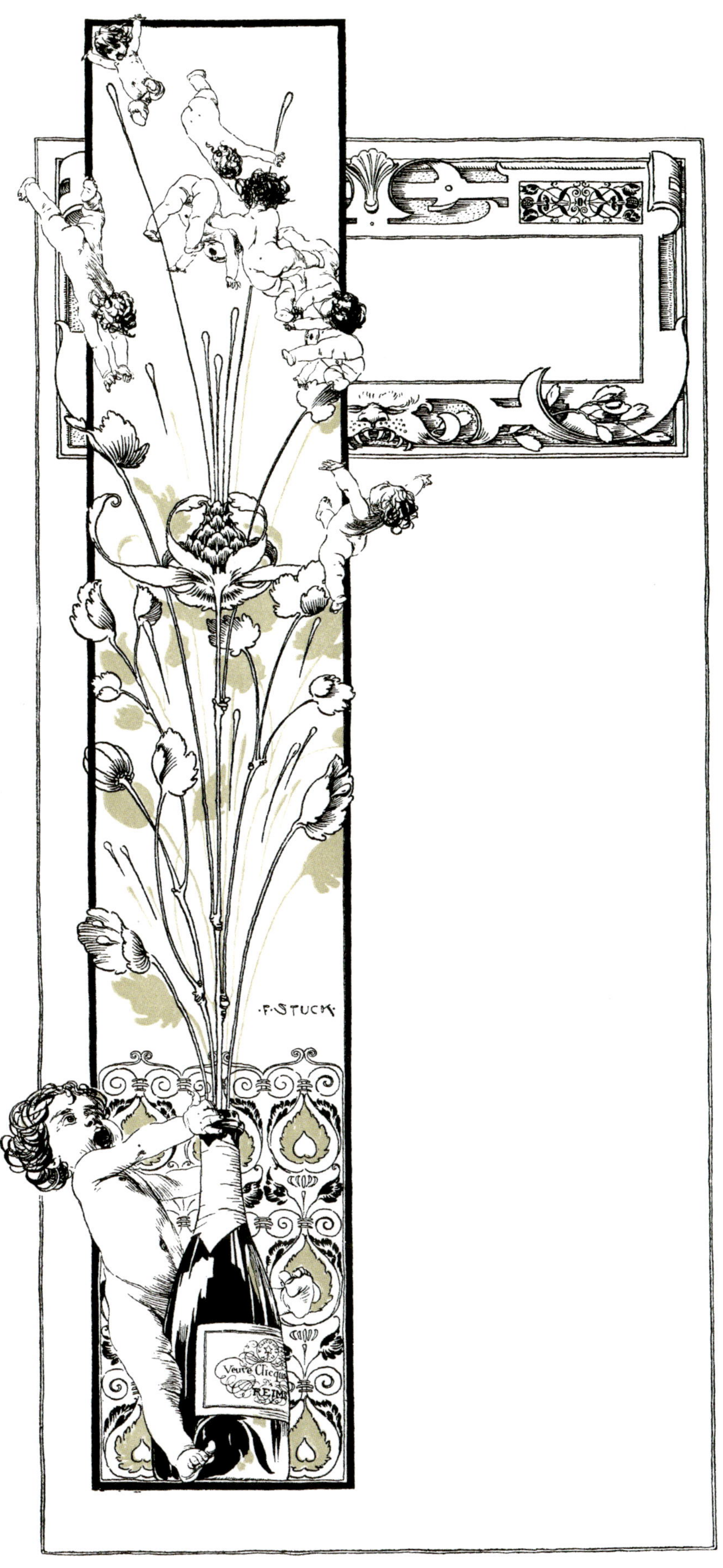

Plate 27

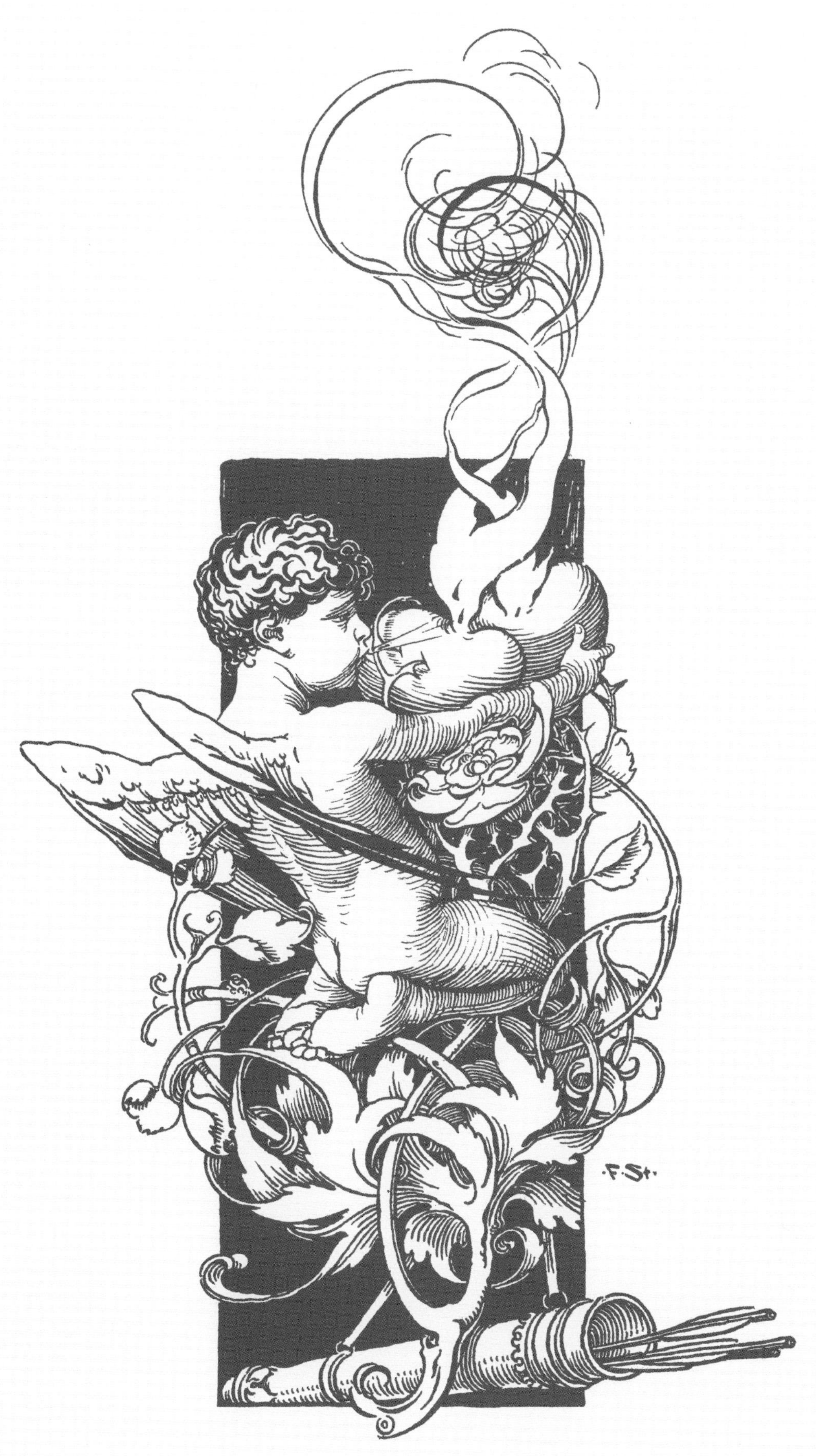
F. St.

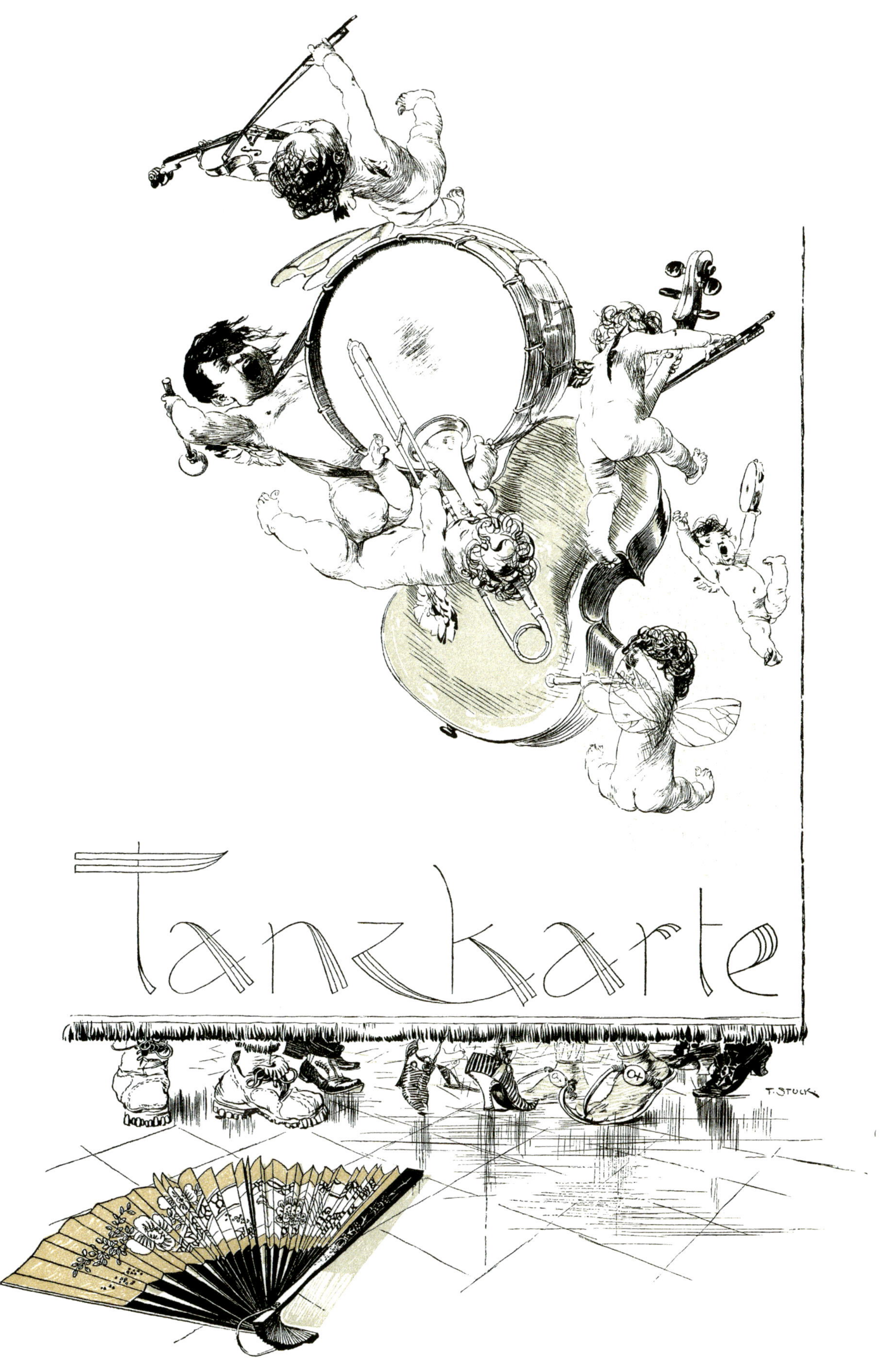
Tanzkarte
T. STUCK

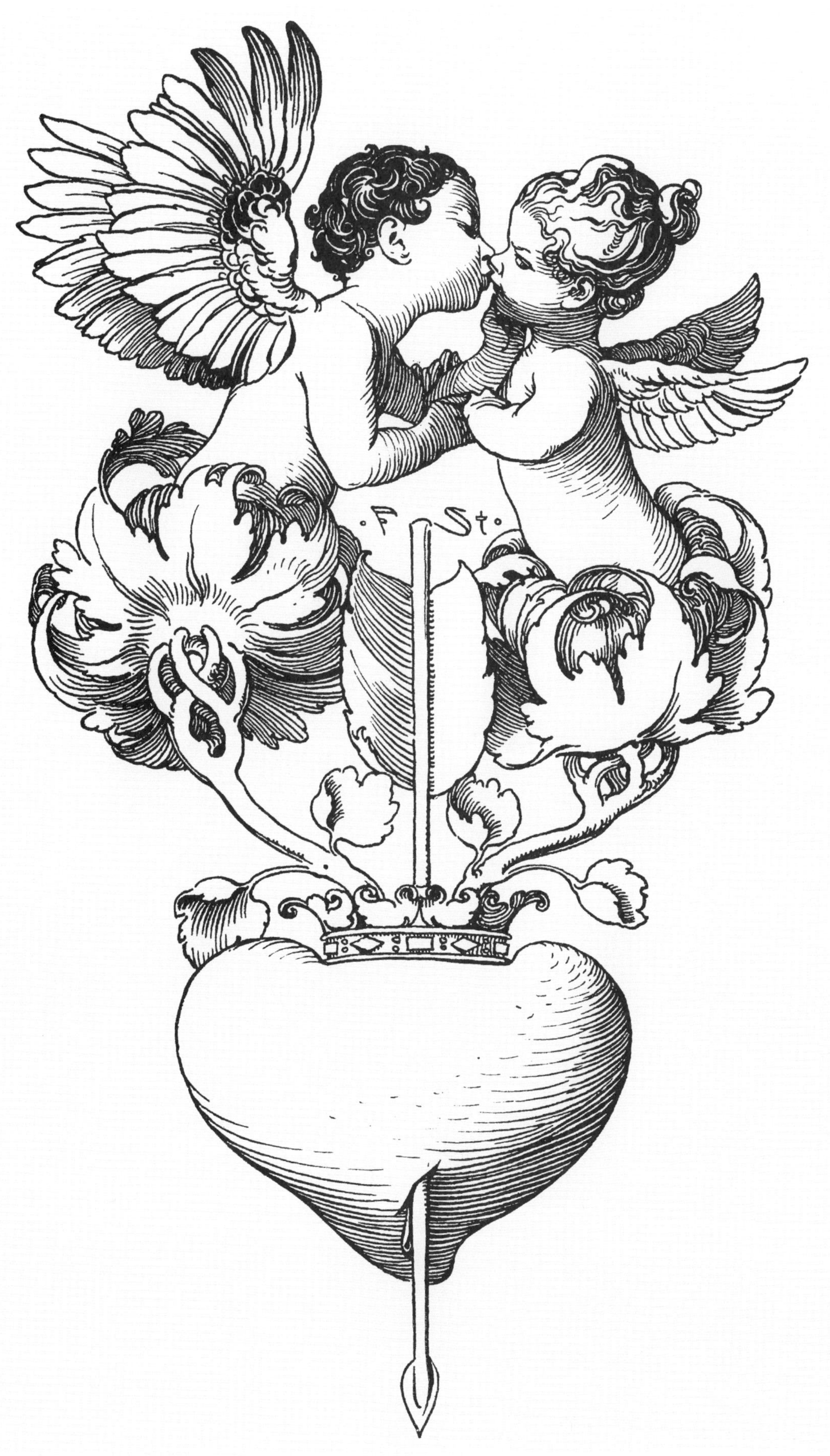
F St

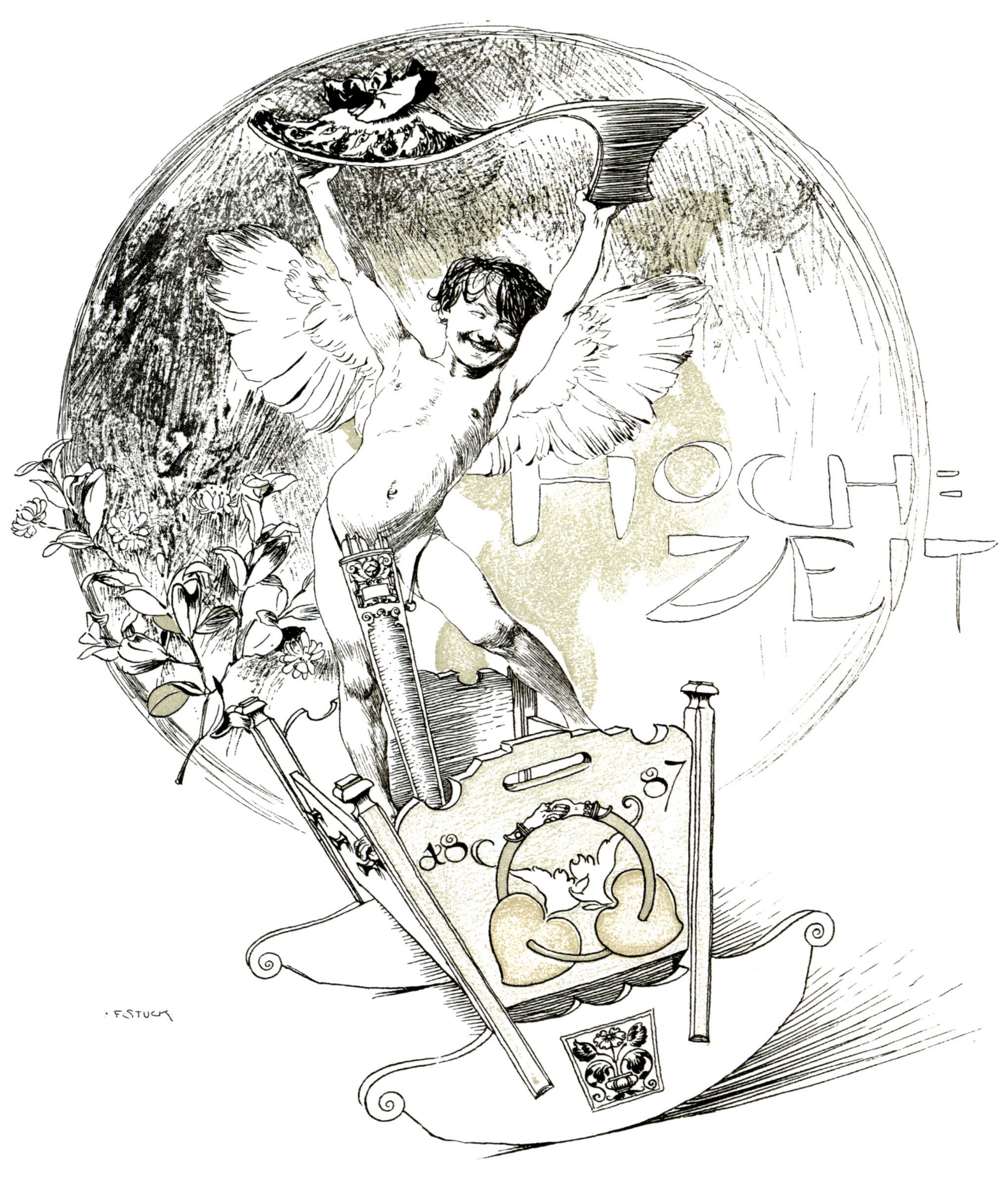
HOCH=
ZEIT
F. STUCK

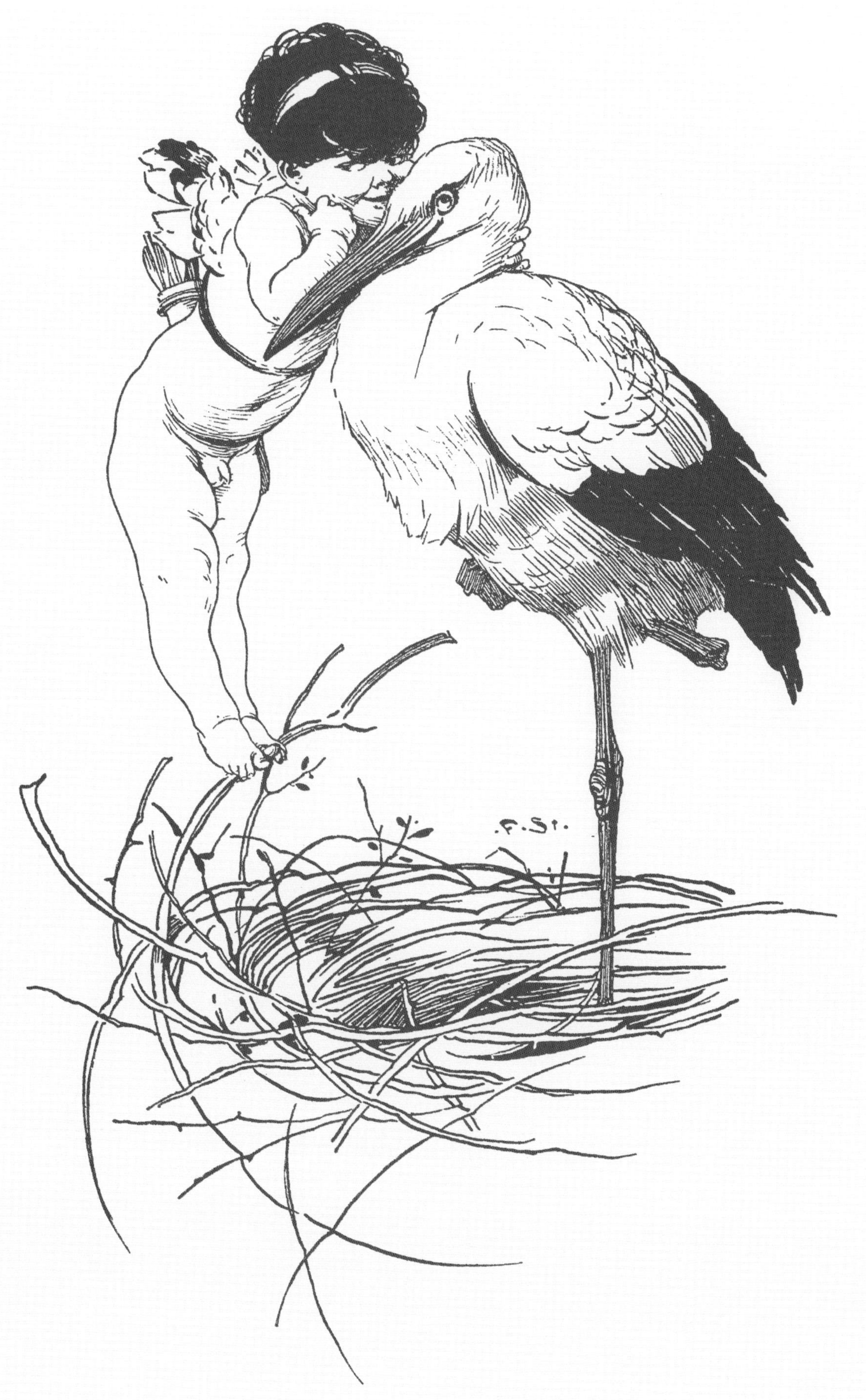

Plate 32

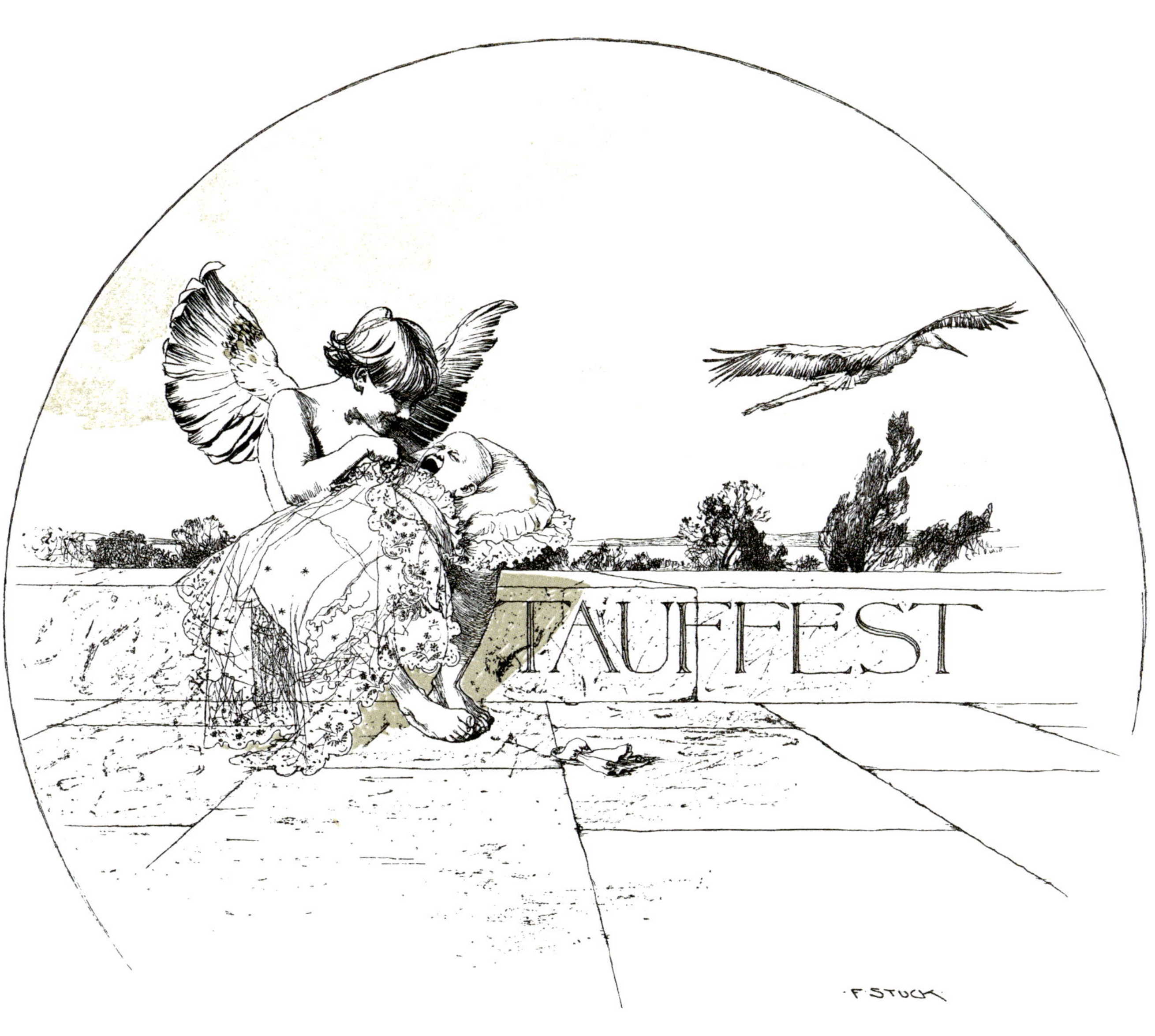
TAUFFEST
F. STUCK

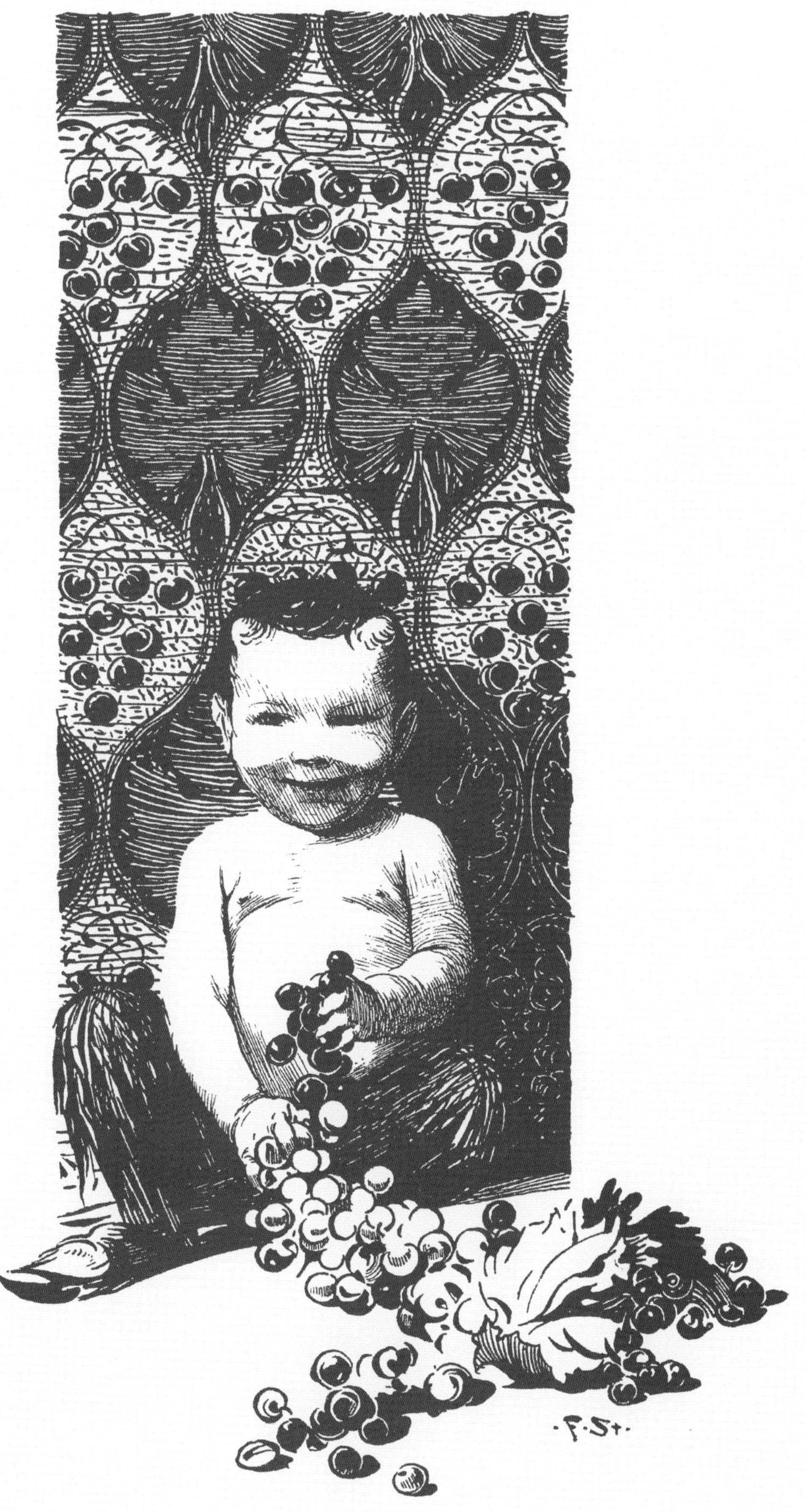

Plate 34

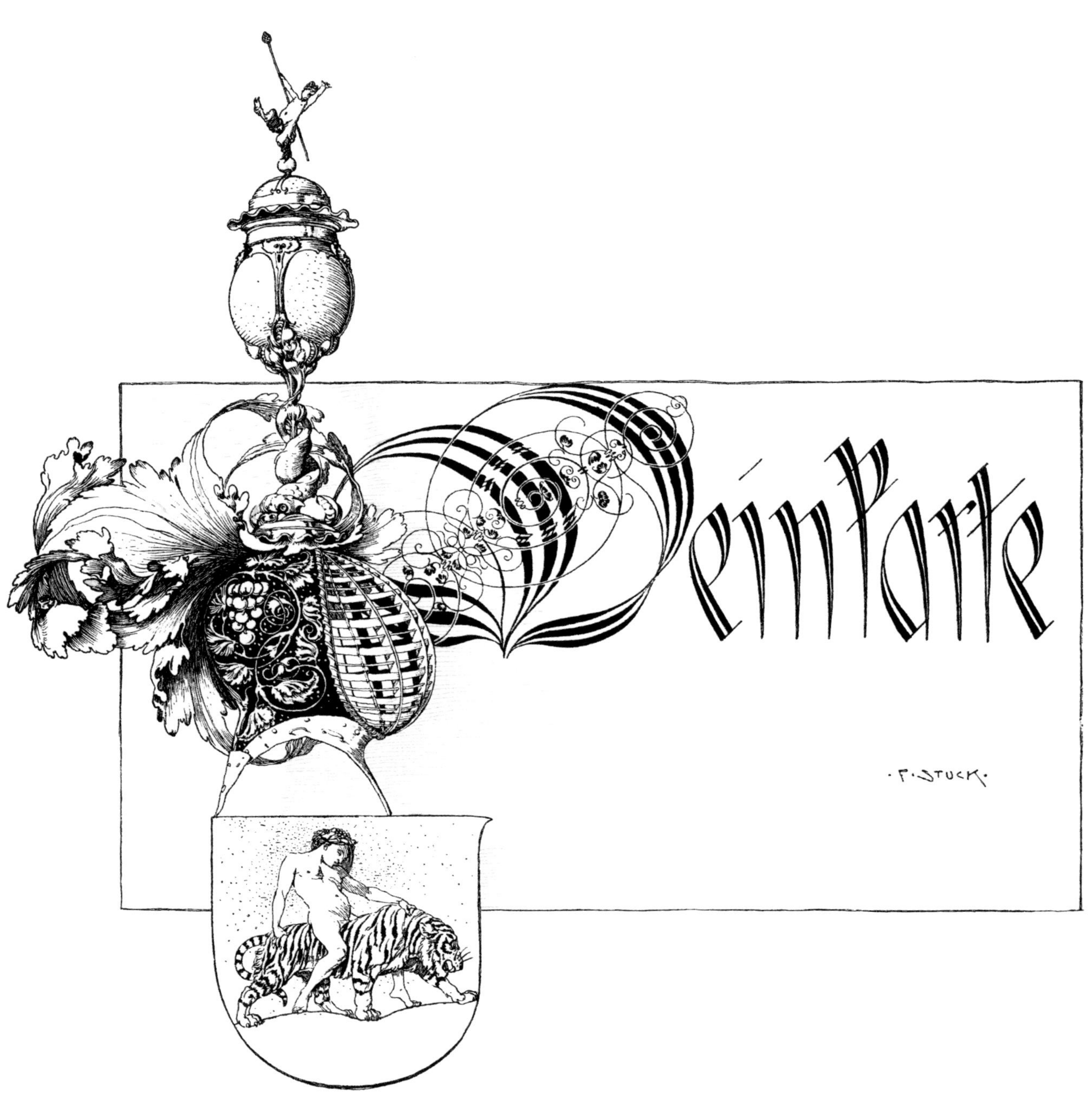

PLATE 35

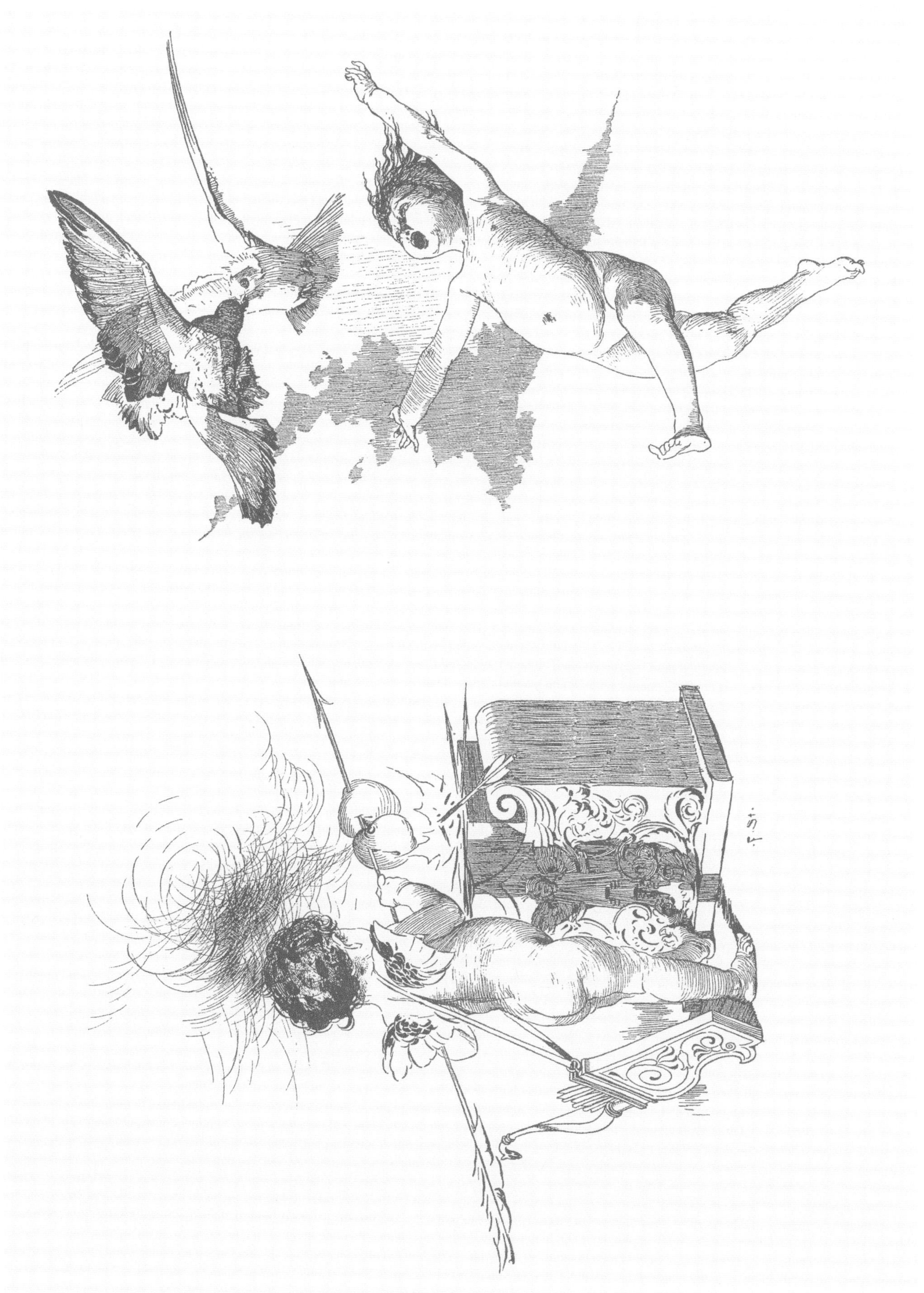

PLATE 36

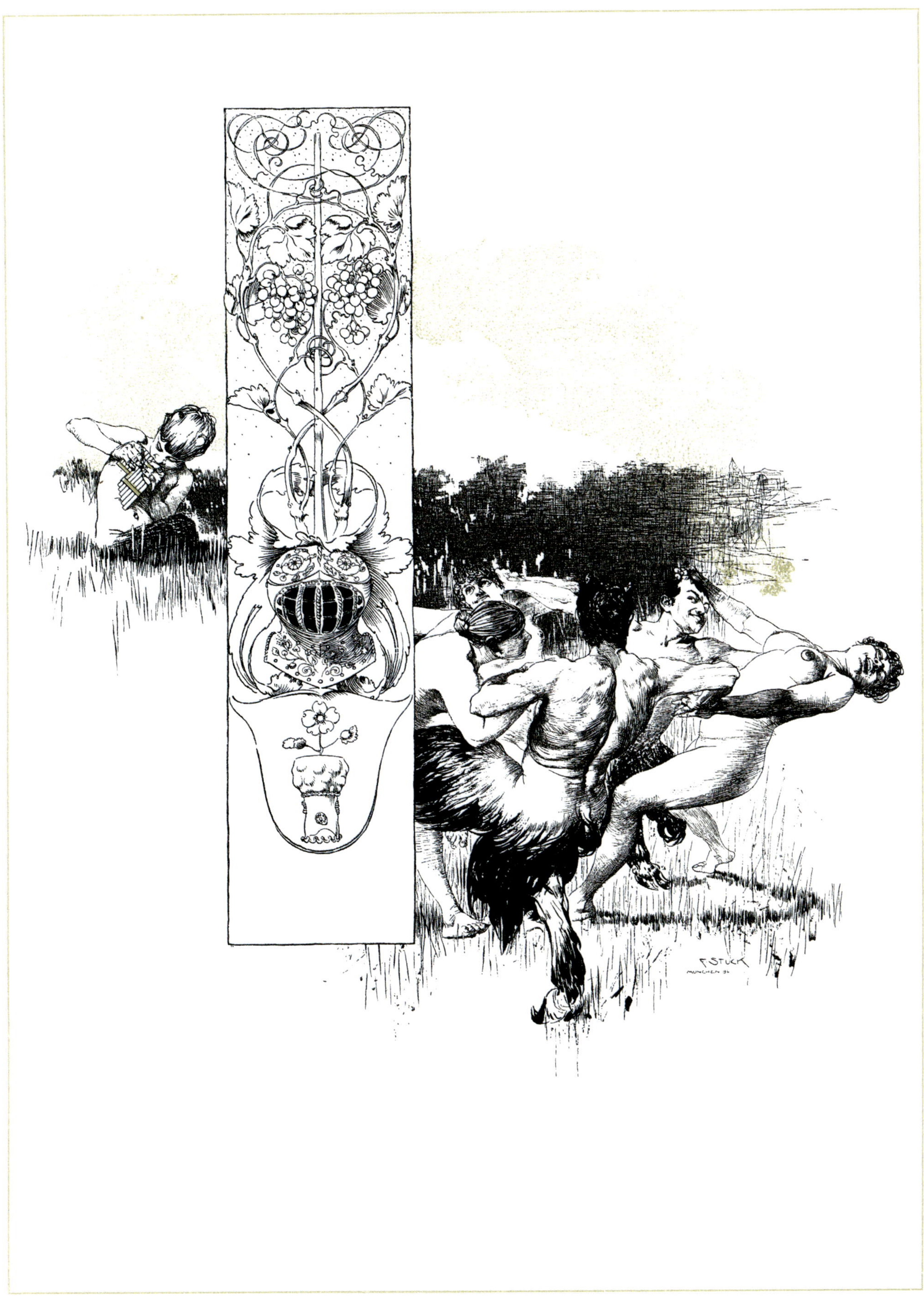

PLATE 37

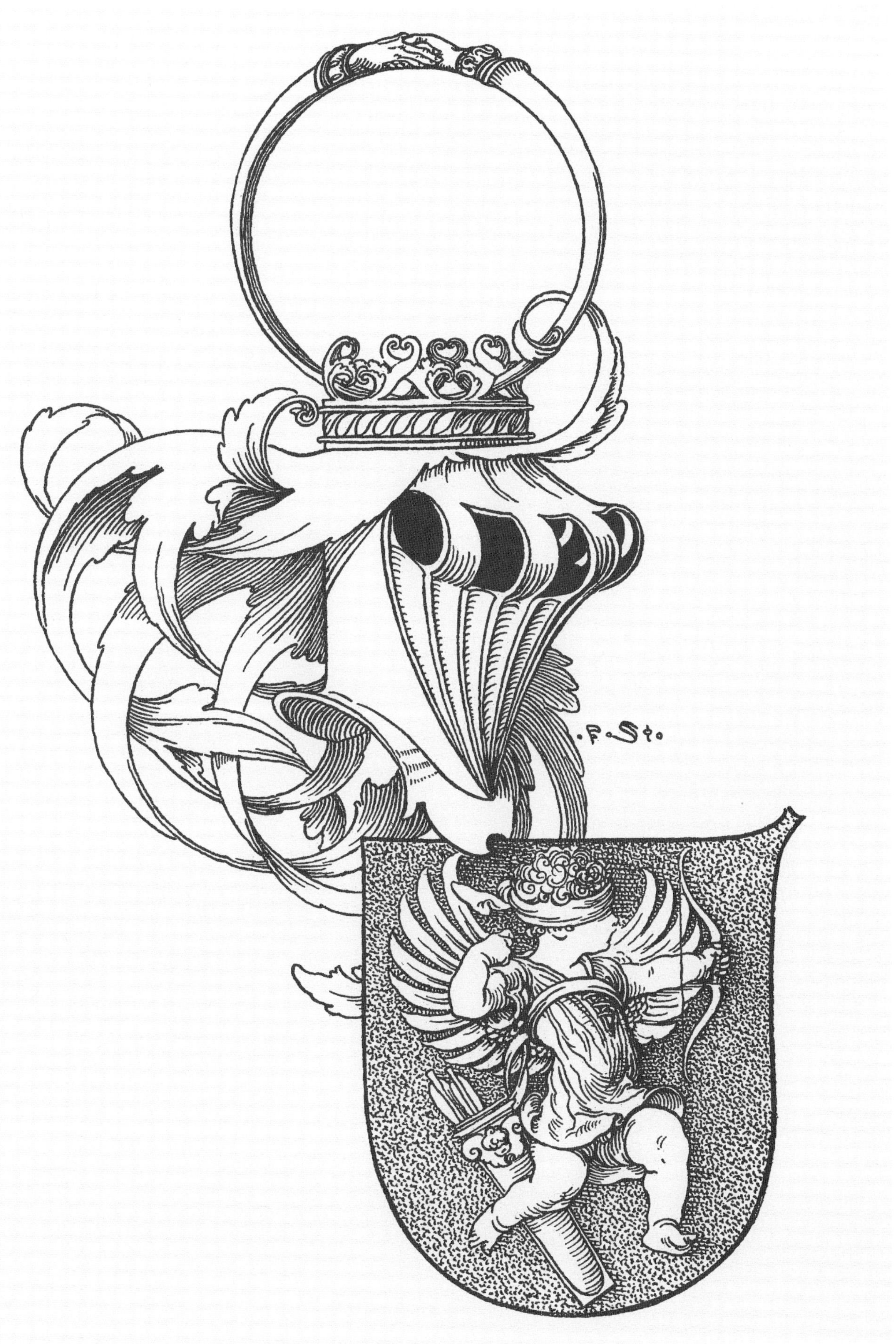

PLATE 38

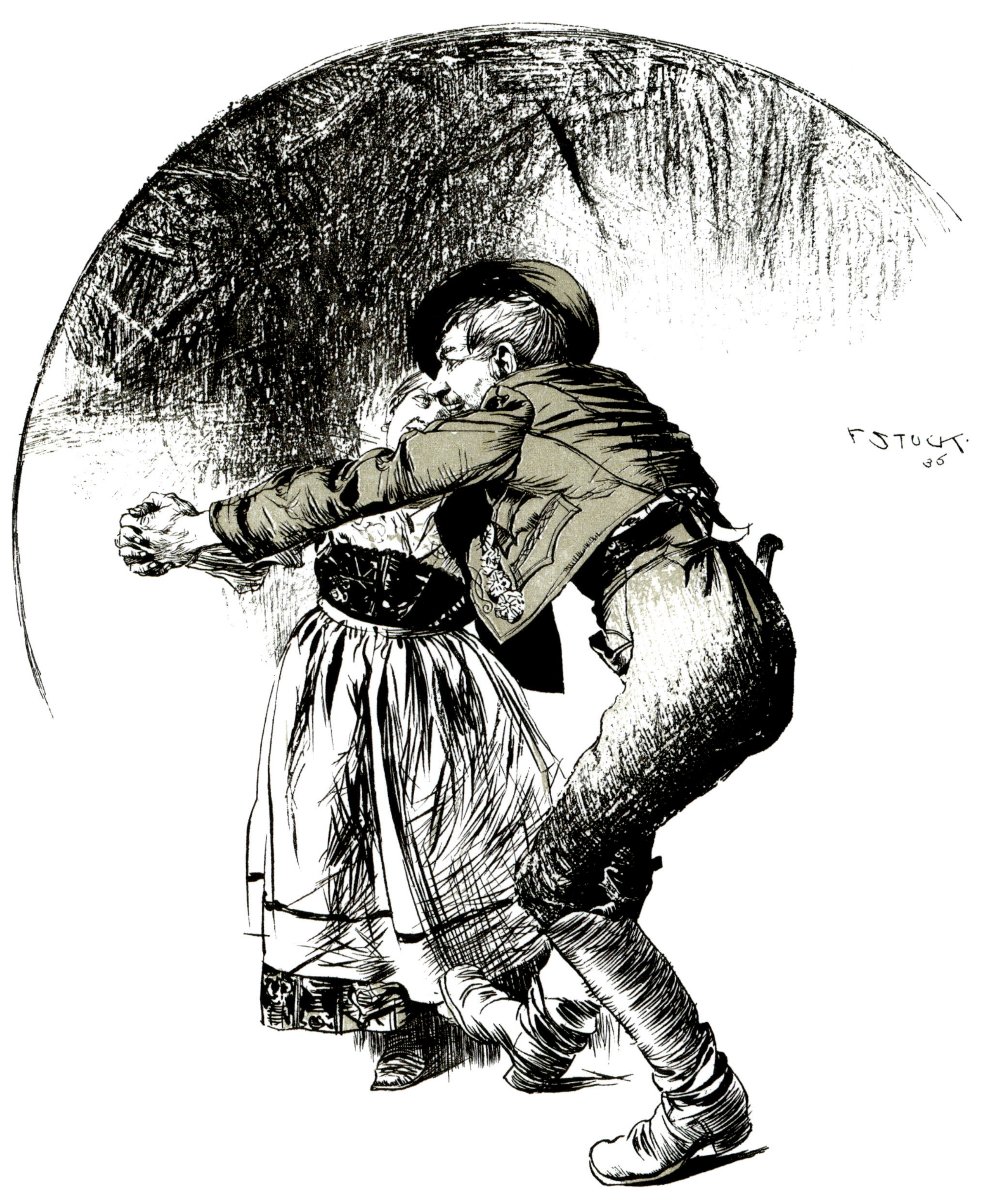
F STUCK
85

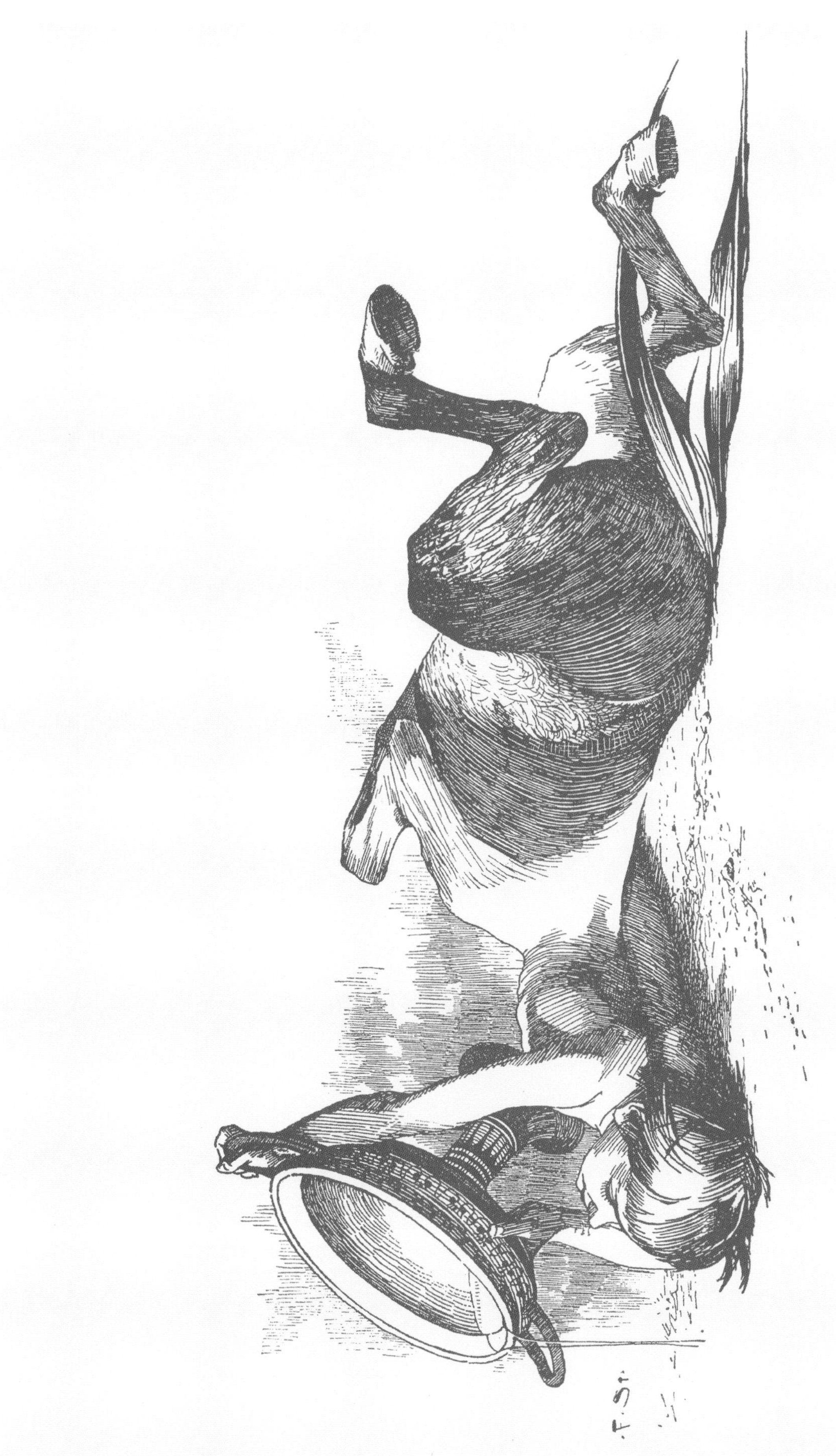

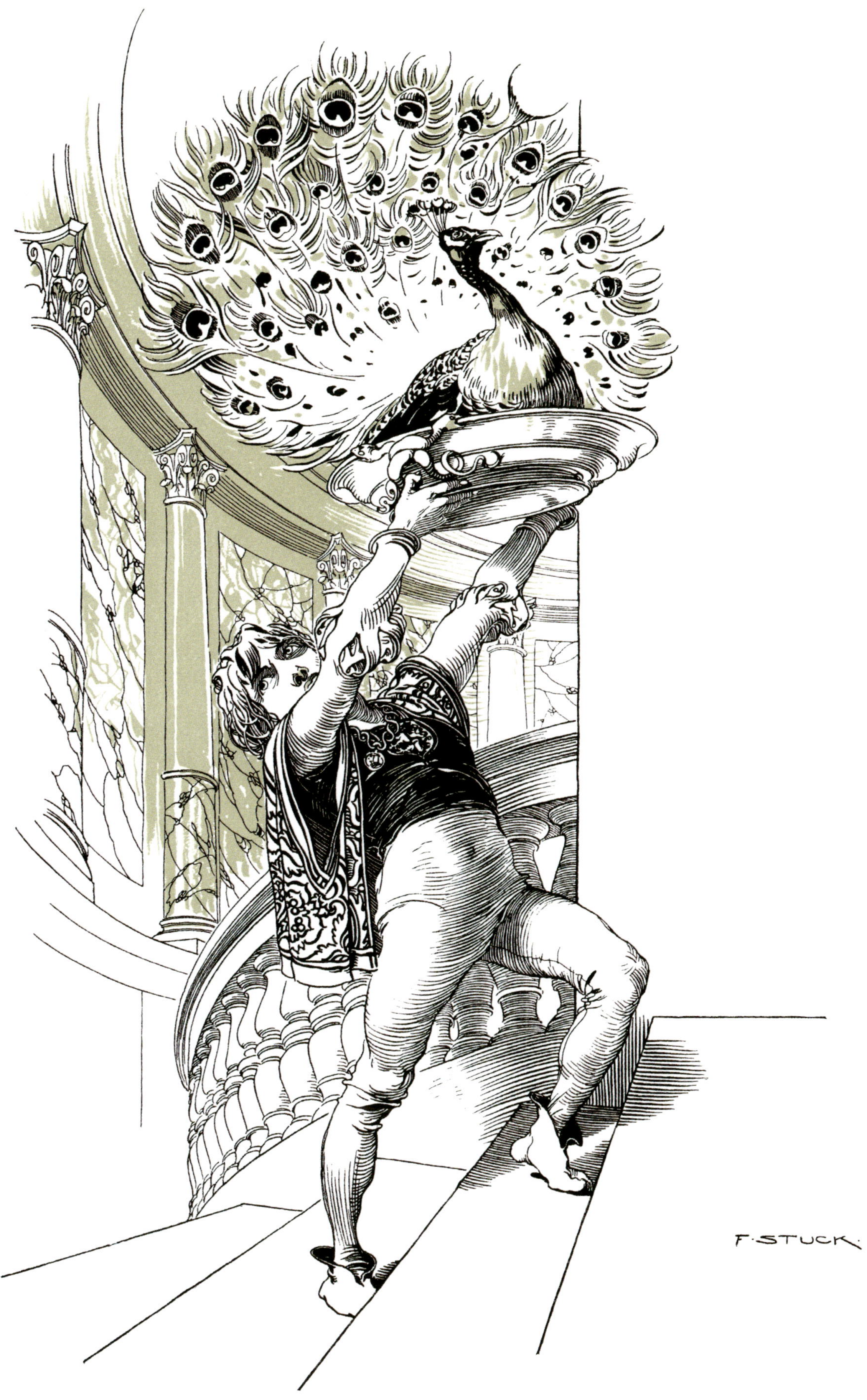

PLATE 41

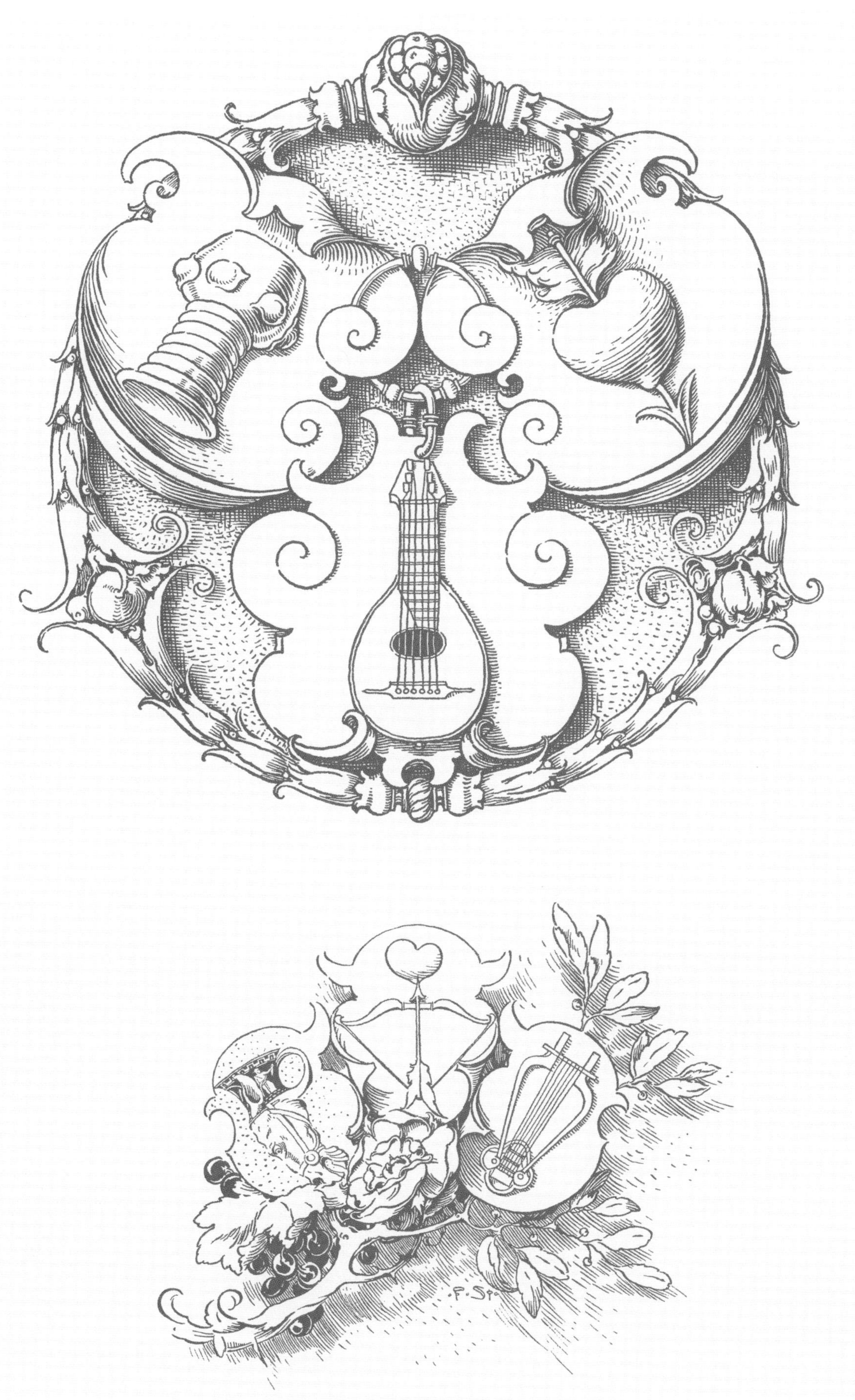

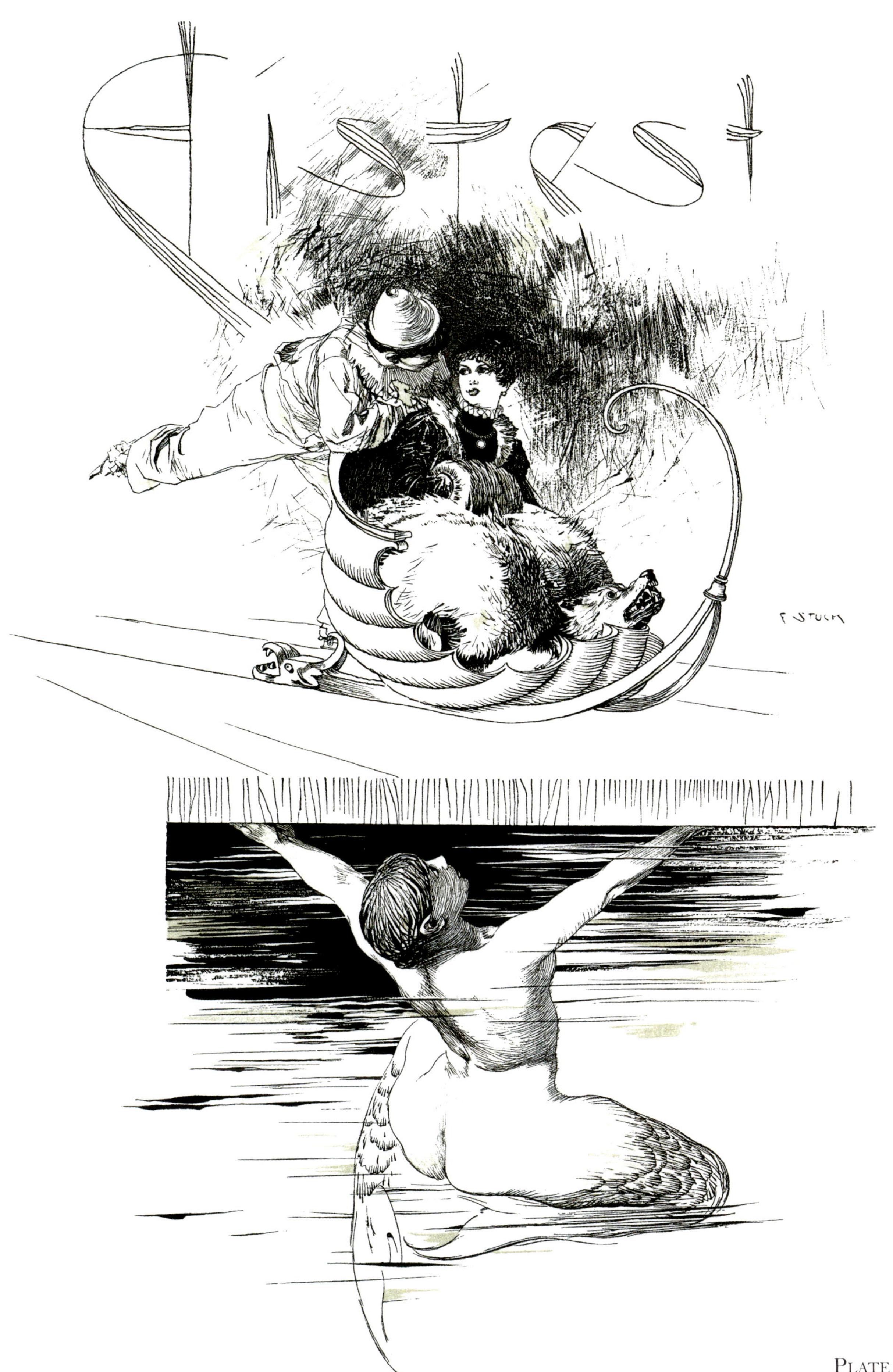
F. STUCK

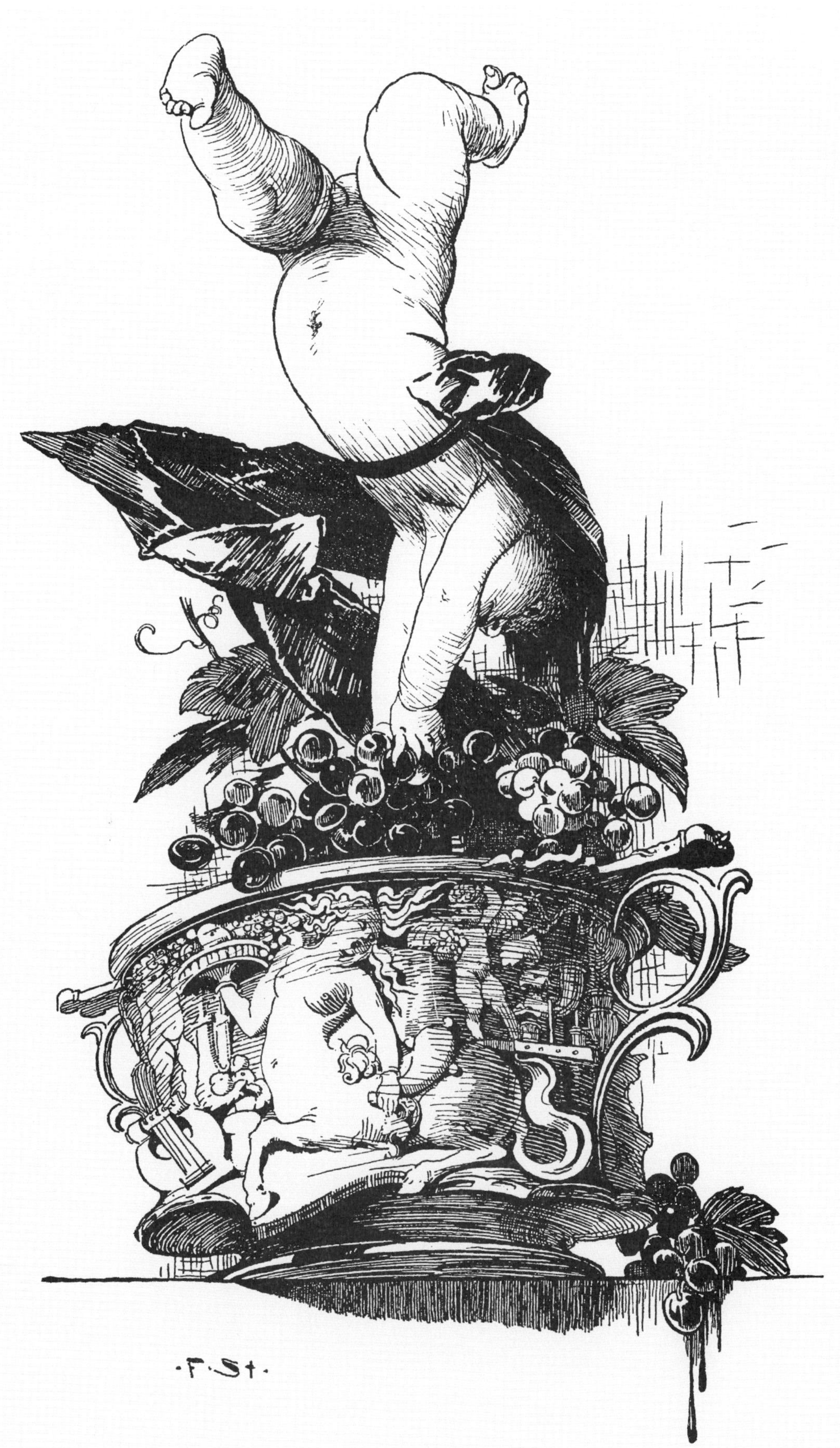

PLATE 44

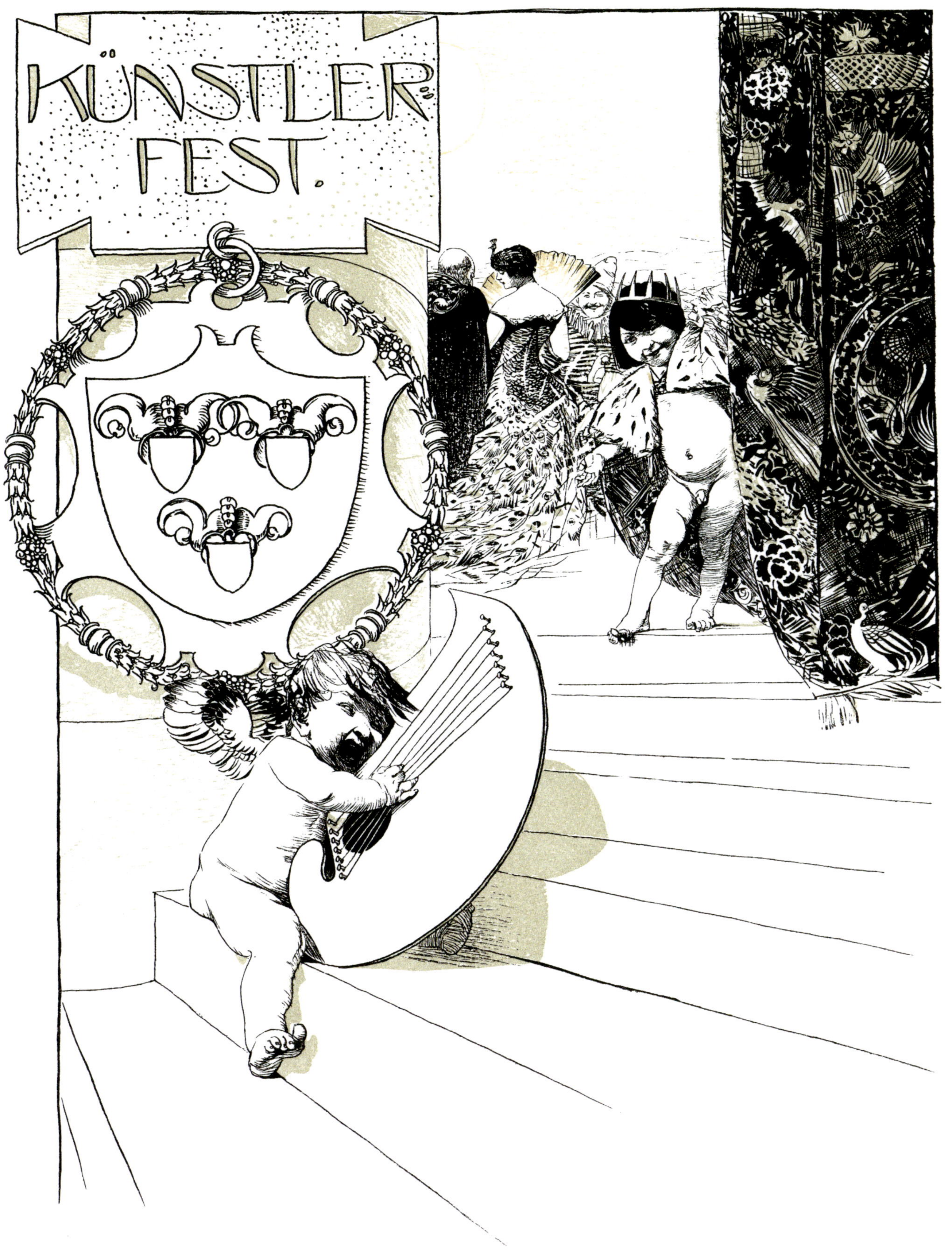
KÜNSTLER
FEST.

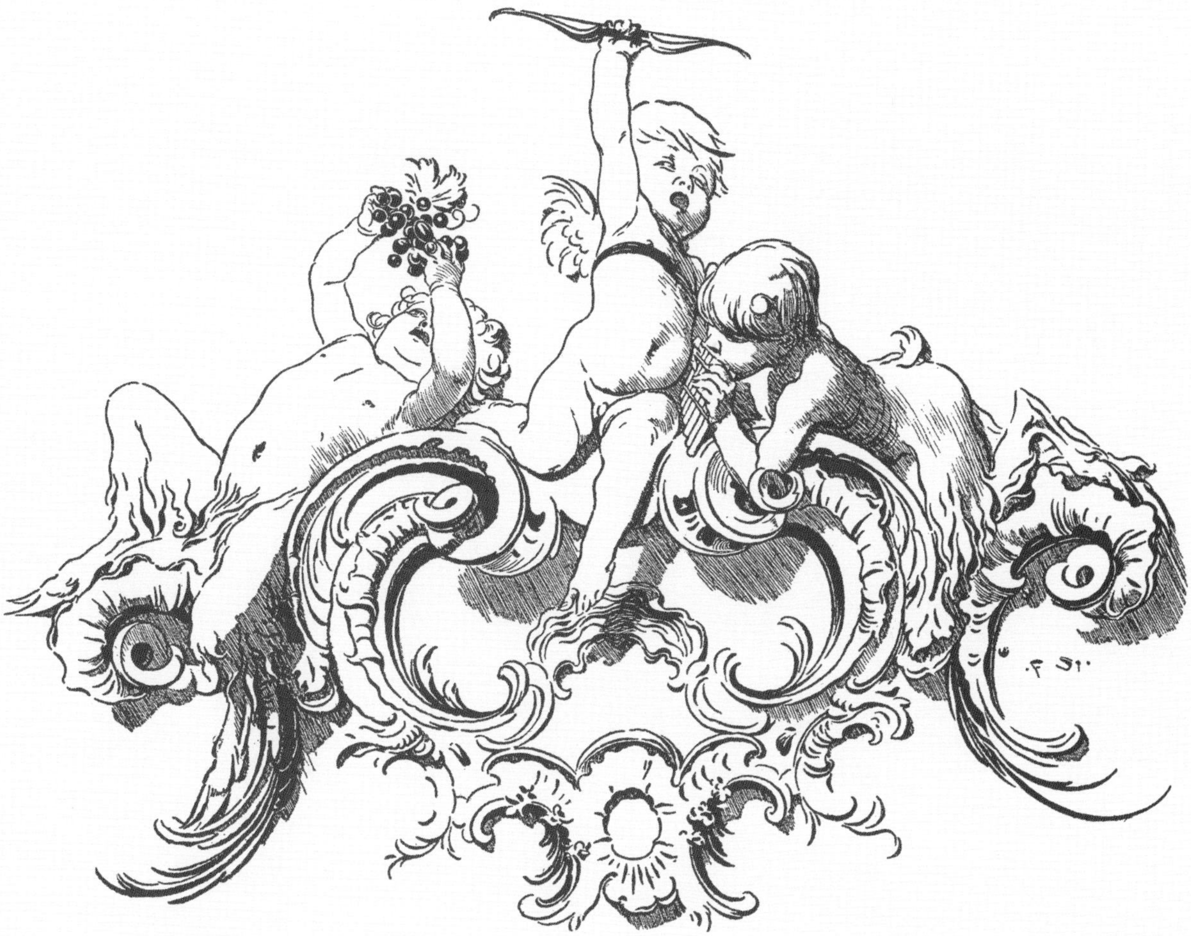

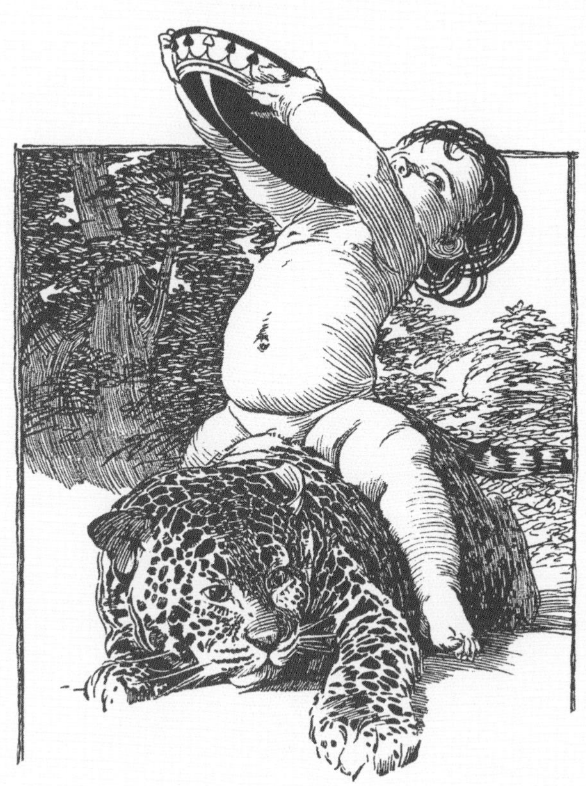

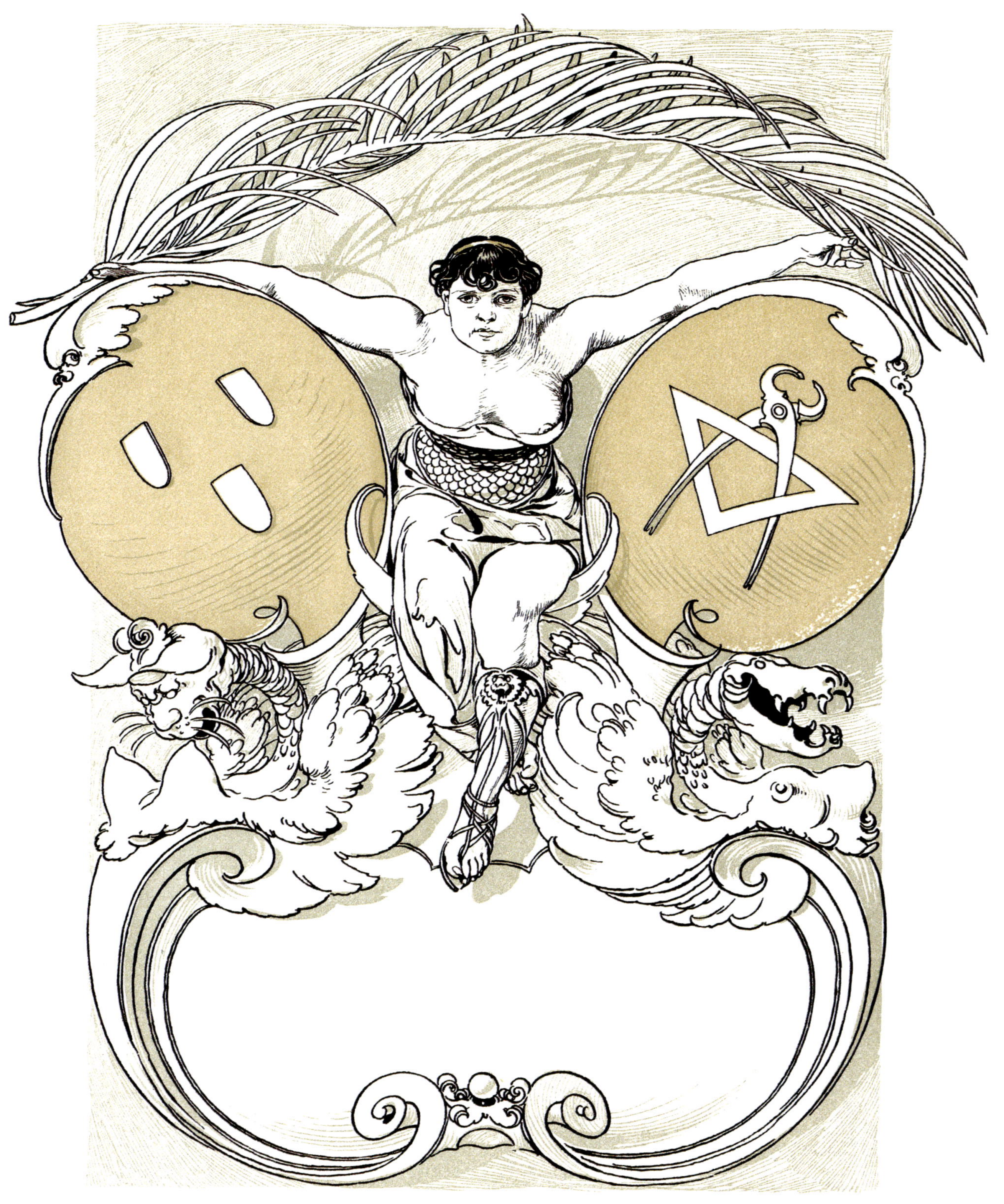

Plate 47

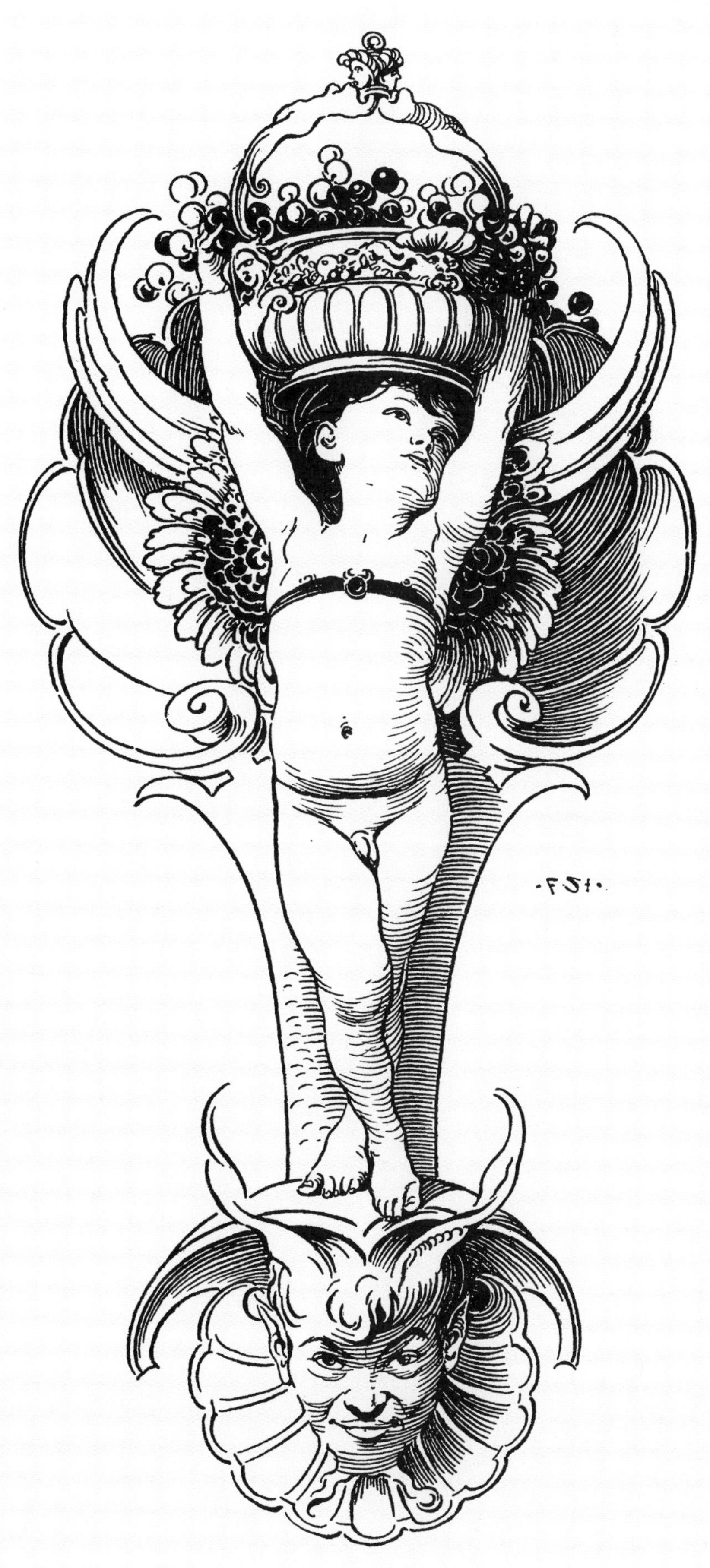

Plate 48

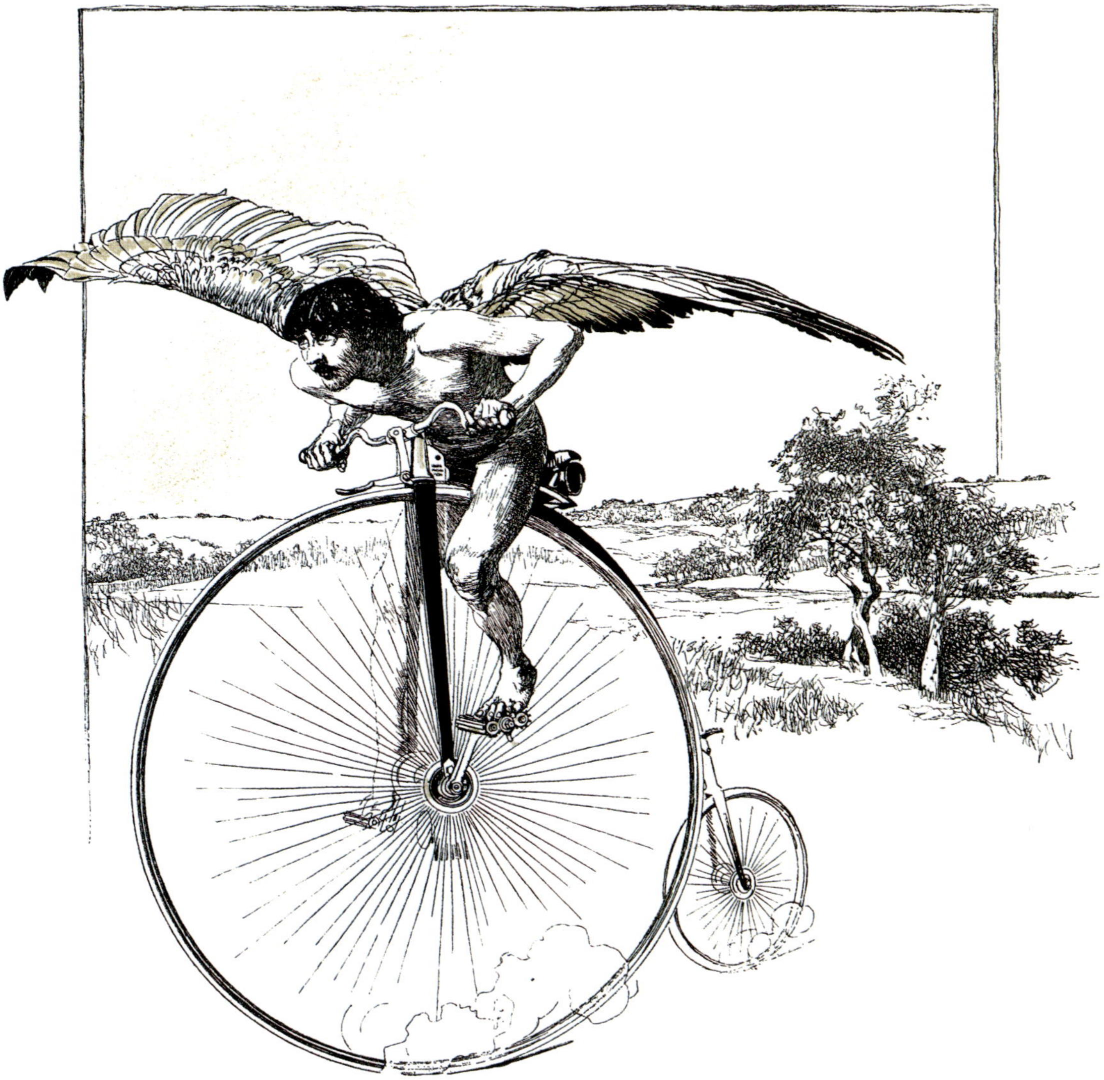

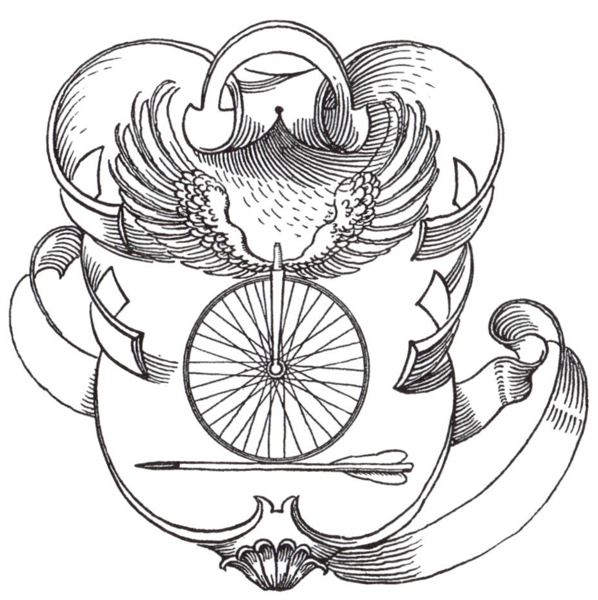

Plate 49

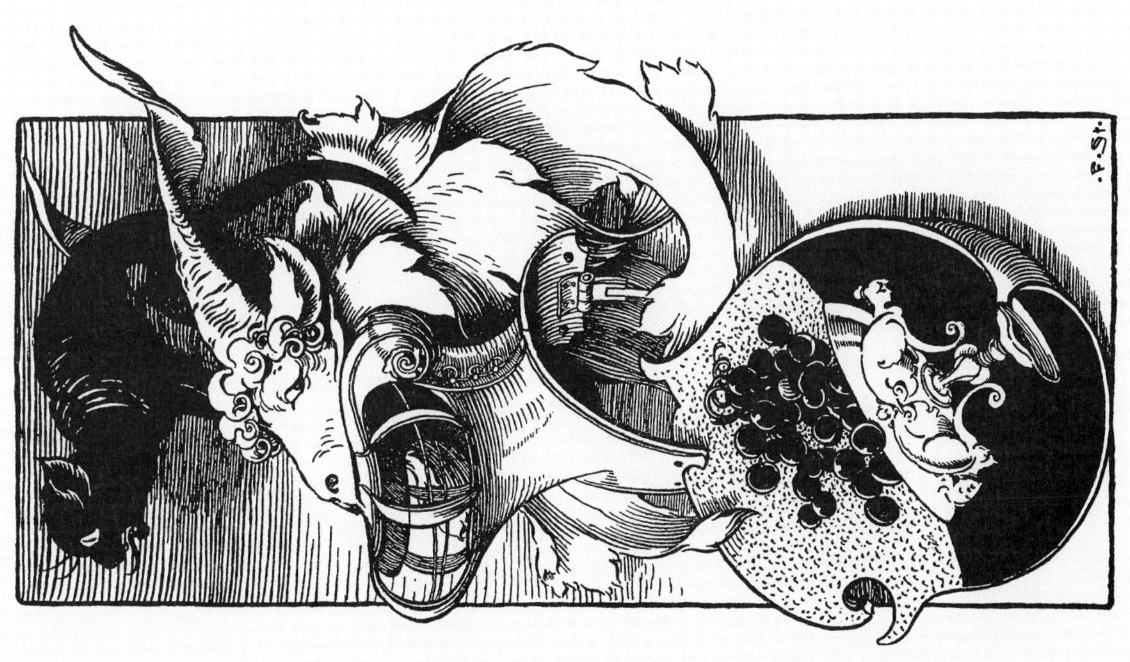

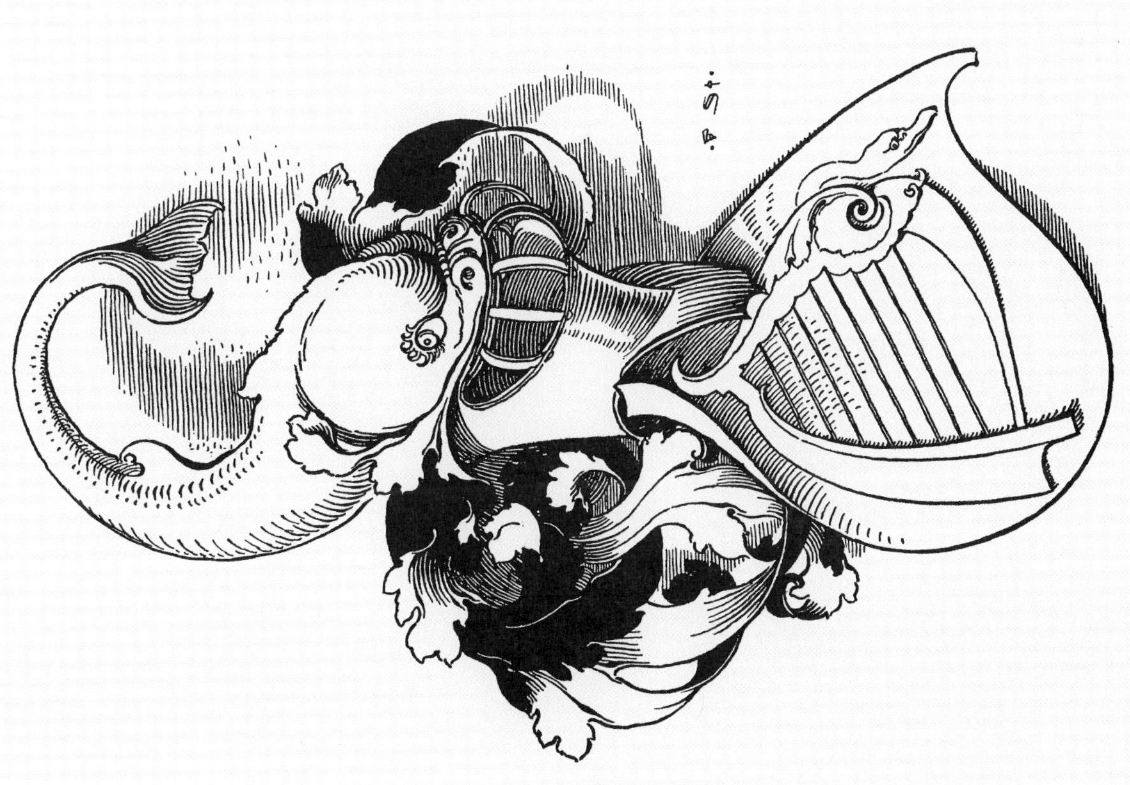